ENGLISH SKILLS FOR UNIVERSITY

Course Book | Workbook | 2B

Terry Phillips
and Anna Phillips

Garnet EDUCATION

Published by
Garnet Publishing Ltd.
8 Southern Court
South Street
Reading RG1 4QS, UK

Copyright © 2012 Garnet Publishing Ltd.

The right of Terry Phillips and Anna Phillips to be identified as the authors of this work has been asserted by them in accordance with the Copyright, Designs and Patents Act 1988.

All rights reserved.
No part of this publication may be reproduced, stored in a retrieval system, or transmitted in any form or by any means, electronic, mechanical, photocopying, recording or otherwise, without the prior permission of the Publisher. Any person who does any unauthorized act in relation to this publication may be liable to criminal prosecution and civil claims for damages.

ISBN 978 1 90757 547 1

British Library Cataloguing-in-Publication Data
A catalogue record for this book is available from the British Library.

Production
Project manager: Kate Kemp
Project consultant: Chris Gough
Editorial team: Lucy Constable, Fiona Dempsey, Kate Kemp
Design: Neil Collier, Mike Hinks
Illustration: Doug Nash
Photography: Banana Stock, Clipart.com, Corbis, Digital Vision, Flat Earth, Getty Images, Image Source, Photodisc, Stockbyte

Every effort has been made to trace the copyright holders and we apologize in advance for any unintentional omissions. We will be happy to insert the appropriate acknowledgements in any subsequent editions.

Audio: Recorded at Motivation Sound Studios (produced by EFS Television Production Ltd) and Silver Street Studios.

Printed and bound
in Lebanon by International Press: interpress@int-press.com

Contents

Book map	4

Course Book

Unit 1: *Culture and Civilization*	7
Unit 2: *They Made Our World*	21
Unit 3: *Media and Literature*	35
Unit 4: *Sports and Leisure*	49
Unit 5: *Nutrition and Health*	63
Review	77

Workbook

Unit 1: *Culture and Civilization*	90
Unit 2: *They Made Our World*	94
Unit 3: *Media and Literature*	98
Unit 4: *Sports and Leisure*	102
Unit 5: *Nutrition and Health*	106
Review	110

Transcripts

Course Book transcript	114
Workbook transcript	133

Word list 141

Book map

Unit	Topic areas	Listening	Speaking	Reading	Writing
1 Culture and Civilization	life events customs life expectancy	understanding new words hearing numbers with decimals	questions using *actually*	understanding commas understanding prepositions	using the present continuous to describe change writing about customs
2 They Made Our World	accidents transport safety	predicting the structure of a talk listening and taking notes	improving your pronunciation describing interrupted actions	predicting the order of information in a text guessing words from context	using the past continuous using *when* with interrupted actions writing a report of an accident conducting and writing about a survey
3 Media and Literature	types of story types of film famous stories in literature	examples and lists listening to a research report	recognizing fact and possibility talking about favourite films conducting a survey	identifying titles and characters understanding summaries of stories	summarizing stories writing about a genre of film
4 Sports and Leisure	types of hobby history of hobbies	recognizing change of subject	talking about a personal hobby using *make* specialist vocabulary giving a talk	skim-reading to check predictions reasons and concessions	using *too* and *also*
5 Nutrition and Health	keeping food fresh food poisoning health advice	using *too much*	referring to graphs and charts using *more, less* and *few* reacting to information	doing research	using *should / shouldn't* + infinitive conditionals expressing fact / possibility

Unit	Vocabulary	Pronunciation	Grammar patterns
1	recognizing superlatives	vowel sounds hard c / soft c	The population of Africa is rising quickly. The children are reading a novel. Life expectancy continued to rise in the 20th century. Calment died in 1997. He gave her a present. The guest gave a present to the woman. When someone dies, the family buys a stone.
2	organizing vocabulary adjectives, nouns and phrasal verbs related to transport	stressing long verbs	What happened? The car was travelling at 80 kph when a wheel broke. / When the wheel broke, the car hit a wall.
3	homophones group words using *say, tell, talk, speak* reflexive pronouns		They were flying at about 50 metres. The pilot checked the height. I saw myself in the mirror.
4	words with more than one meaning adjectives ending in *~ing* and *~ed*	unstressed syllables	It is very big. It is not strong enough.
5	countable and uncountable nouns	weak forms of common grammatical words	You shouldn't smoke. If you live in a hot country, you need more water. If you lie in the sun, you will probably develop skin cancer.

Unit 1
Culture and Civilization

Key vocabulary

anniversary (n)
average (adj/n)
be born (v)
birth (n)
birthday (n)
birth rate (n)
blow out (candles) (v)
celebrate (v)
ceremony (n)
christening (n)
costume (n)
custom (n)
death (n)
death rate (n)
die (v)
event (n)

falling population (n)
fireworks (n)
firework display (n)
funeral (n)
get married (v)
growth (n)
guest (n)
happen (v)
honeymoon (n)
life expectancy (n)
make a speech (v)
marriage (n)
occasion (n)
parade (n)
present (n)
rising population (n)

speech (n)
wedding (n)

Unit 1 Culture and Civilization

Lesson 1: Listening

A Study the pictures then answer the questions.
1. What is the connection between the three pictures?
2. What is happening in each picture?

B Listen.
1. 1:1 Match each sentence to a life event.
2. 1:2 Listen again. Identify a key word or phrase for each life event.
3. Add the words and phrases to the table.

Table 1

life event	ceremony	customs
birth	christening	
marriage		man puts ring on finger of bride's left hand
death		

C 1:3 Listen to a short lecture about life and culture in the UK. Make notes in the *customs* column of the table.

D Study the words below from the lecture. Did you understand them in context?
- soft toy
- bride
- the best man
- gravestone

E Do you have the same customs in your culture?

Skills Check 1

Understanding new words
- You can often understand new words from the context.
  Example:
  He puts a **ring** on the bride's finger.
  so *ring* =

- Sometimes a lecturer explains a new word.
  Example:
  During the wedding ceremony, the **groom** – that's the **man** who is **getting married** …

OBJECTIVES
- understand new words
- recognize superlatives
- hear numbers with decimals

F Look at the sentences below.

1 Complete each sentence with a word from the box.

| birth | death | marriage |

  a. Cuba has a very high _____ rate at 17.7 per 1,000 people.
  b. Africa is the continent with the highest _____ rate at 14 per 1,000 people.
  c. The _____ rate in North America is 14 per 1,000 people, while in South America it is 21.5.

2 🔊 **1:4** Listen and check.

G Look at Table 1. Work in pairs.

1 🔊 **1:5** Listen and write numbers in the boxes.

Student 1: Complete the green boxes.
Student 2: Complete the blue boxes.

2 Exchange information to complete the table.

H Study Table 2. The information is not in order. Which continent do you think has:

1 the highest birth rate?
2 the highest death rate?
3 the fastest population growth rate?
4 the lowest birth rate?
5 the lowest death rate?
6 the lowest population growth rate?

I Look at Table 2. Work in pairs.

1 🔊 **1:6** Listen and write numbers in the boxes.

Student 1: Complete the green boxes.
Student 2: Complete the blue boxes.

2 Exchange information to complete the table.

J Look at Table 2.

1 Which continents have a rising population?
2 Which continents have a falling population?
3 🔊 **1:7** Listen and check.
4 Complete the *difference* column.

K Do you know the birth, death and marriage rates in your country?

Table 1: *Marriage rates around the world (per 000)*

Country	Marriages
Cuba	
Philippines	14.2
Bangladesh	
Egypt	
USA	
Syria	
China	
UK	
France	
Argentina	

Table 2: *Birth rates and death rates by continent (per 000)*

Continent	Births	Deaths	Difference
Africa			
Europe			
North America			
South America			
Asia			
Australasia			

Skills Check 2

Hearing numbers with decimals

Study the pronunciation of the decimal number below:

2.5

two **point** five

In fast speech, some consonant sounds are not pronounced. Compare the examples below:

8.3

eigh(t) **poin(t)** three

2.1

two **point** one

Lesson 2: Speaking

A Look at the three pictures. What are the life events?

1 What is happening?

2 Where is the event happening?

B 🔊 1:8 Listen to part of a tutorial. Which event above are they talking about?

C Study the words in the box.

| celebration | costumes | dance | ~~festival~~ | figures | graves |
| graveyards | parades | popular | prayers | relatives |

1 Did you hear them in the tutorial? Did you understand from the context?

2 Look at this extract from the tutorial. Write a word from the box in each space.

> S1: I researched a _festival_. It's called the Day of the Dead.
> S2: Is it a funeral?
> S1: No, not really. It's a day to remember dead friends and _____.
> S2: Does it happen every year?
> S1: Yes, that's right. It's on the first and second of November.
> S2: Where does it happen?
> S1: In Mexico, certainly, but I think it happens in Nicaragua and so on.
> S2: Is it _____?
> S1: Yes, very popular.
> S2: What happens exactly?
> S1: People visit _____ and say _____. They tell stories, they sing and they _____. They go to the _____. They often take the favourite food and drink of the dead person. They take toys for dead children.
> S2: So, is it a _____?
> S1: Yes, exactly. It's a day to be happy. There are _____ through the streets. People wear _____ or carry _____ of dead people.
> S2: When did the custom start?
> S1: I understand that it started hundreds of years ago, at the time of the Aztecs.

3 🔊 1:9 Listen to the tutorial again and check your answers.

OBJECTIVES	• talk about customs	• ask questions with the correct form
	• learn and use typical conversational expressions	

D Study the questions.

1 Correct each question.
   a. It is a funeral?   *Is it a funeral?*
   b. Does it happens every year?
   c. What does happen exactly?
   d. Are they a celebration?
   e. When started the custom?
   f. Is popular?

2 1:10 Listen and check your ideas.

3 Practise the questions.

E Study the sentences and phrases.

1 Complete each phrase with one word in the space.
   a. No, not *really*.
   b. Yes, that's _____.
   c. In Mexico, _____.
   d. Yes, _____ popular.
   e. What happens _____?
   f. I _____ that it started hundreds of years ago.

2 1:11 Listen and check your ideas.

3 Practise the sentences and phrases.

F You are going to take part in a tutorial.

1 Work in pairs.
   Student A: Look at notes A.
   Student B: Look at notes B.

A
wedding customs in India
wedding lasts many days
100 to 1,000 guests
= friends, family, people from village
cost = £30,000
many marriages are arranged
= parents choose bridegroom

B
birth customs in Muslim countries
v. old – 1,400 yrs
father speaks into baby's right ear
gives baby something sweet
cuts baby's hair
weighs the hair, e.g., 1 gram
gives weight in silver to poor people

2 Do the research. Follow the advice in Skills Check 3.

3 Role-play a tutorial. Use some of the expressions in Exercise E.

Skills Check 1

Questions: Revision

1 *yes/no* questions
Is it popular?
Are they happy?
Does it happen in the USA?
Do people dance?

2 Information questions
Where **does it happen**?
When **did it start**?

Remember!
What **happens**?
What ~~does~~ happen?

Skills Check 2

actually
We use *actually* to correct someone politely.

We can put it at the beginning or the end of a sentence.

Examples:
Actually, Mexico's in Central America – not South America.
Mexico's in Central America, **actually**.

Skills Check 3

Doing research
You often have to do research for a tutorial. Make sure you can answer key questions about your research.
Who …?
Where …?
When …?
What …?
How much …?
How many …?
Why …?

Look up any new words in a dictionary. Make sure you:
• know the meaning(s).
• can pronounce the word(s).

Lesson 3: Vocabulary and Pronunciation

A Study the photographs and the noun phrases in the box.

1 Find each item in the box in the photographs above.

2 Mark the stress in each multi-syllable word.

3 🎧 **1:12** Listen and check your answers.

> a cake   a christening
> a costume   a honeymoon
> a parade   a present
> candles   fireworks
> a speech   an anniversary

B Match each verb below with one of the noun phrases in the box.

1 Write the noun phrase after the verb.
   a. take part in   _a parade_
   b. cut   _____
   c. go to   _____
   d. go on   _____
   e. wear   _____
   f. blow out   _____
   g. give   _____
   h. watch   _____
   i. make   _____

2 🎧 **1:13** Listen and check.

3 Talk about the photographs. Use some of the phrases above.

C Ask and answer questions about customs in your country.

1 Use the information to make questions.
   a. children blow out candles / birthday parties?
   b. bride / groom / cut / cake together?
   c. people / fireworks / New Year?
   d. most people christen / babies?
   e. when / people / parades?
   f. when / people / costume?
   g. what / presents / give / bride / groom?
   h. where / people / honeymoon?
   i. who / speech / wedding?
   j. when / celebrate / anniversary?

2 🎧 **1:14** Listen and repeat the questions.

12   English Skills for University 2b, Course Book, Unit 1

OBJECTIVES
- revise and develop vocabulary related to customs and ceremonies
- practise pronunciation of vowel sounds
- practise pronunciation of hard and soft c

D Look at the green box.

How do you pronounce the letter c in each word?

1 Say each word.
2 🎧 1:15 Listen and check.
3 When is c hard? When is it soft?
4 How do you pronounce the words in the blue box?
5 🎧 1:16 Listen and check.

| culture | civilization | custom | called |
| costume | ceremony | celebrate | close |

| Catholic | cemetery | circus | confetti |
| Cupid | create | clap | |

Skills Check

Saying c

We pronounce c as:

1 a hard sound = /k/ before a, o, u
2 a soft sound = /s/ before e, i
3 a hard sound = /k/ in front of consonants

Examples:
cat, cost, cut, celebrate, city, clothes, cross

E Saying vowels.

Is the vowel the same (S) or different (D) in each pair of words?

1 Say the words and write S or D.

a.	weigh	rate	S
b.	death	guest	
c.	bride	dies	
d.	grave	prayer	
e.	born	groom	
f.	birth	church	

2 🎧 1:17 Listen and check.
3 Practise the words.

F Look at the conversations.

1 🎧 1:18 Listen to the conversations.
2 🎧 1:19 Listen and repeat.
3 Practise the conversations in pairs.

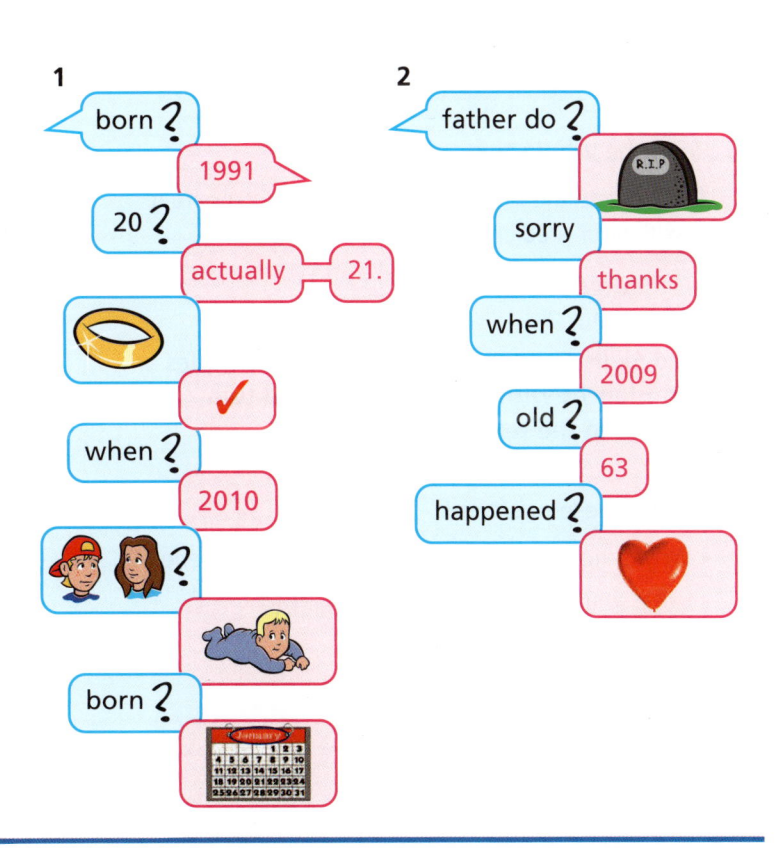

Lesson 4: Reading

A Read the introduction to the text opposite. Choose the correct heading below and write it in the space at the top of the text.

a. **When will I get married?**

b. **How long will I live for?**

c. **How many children will I have?**

d. **Will I ever be rich?**

B Look at Table 1 on the opposite page. Predict the average age of death for each period in history.

C Follow the reading steps.

1 Read the first paragraph and answer the questions below.
   a. What kind of dangers do you think there were in prehistoric times?
   b. Which two great civilizations had the same life expectancy?

2 Read the second paragraph. What affected life expectancy during the Middle Ages?

3 Read paragraphs 3–5. Why did life expectancy improve:
   • in the Victorian Age?
   • from 1900 CE–1950 CE?
   • from 1950 CE–2000 CE?

4 When will average life expectancy be 100?

D Read the whole text.

1 Complete the information in Table 1. Compare it with your predictions.

2 Complete the line graph (Figure 1).

E Read Skills Check 1. Then find more examples of sentences with single commas and two commas in the text.

F Discuss these questions.
   • Why is life expectancy rising more slowly in general?
   • What is life expectancy in your country?

Skills Check 1
Understanding commas
- A single comma joins **two pieces** of information in the same sentence.
- Two commas give **extra information** about the subject or object.
- You can often ignore information in two commas and still understand the text.

Skills Check 2
Understanding prepositions
- Prepositions often come before a noun or noun phrase.
- Join each preposition to its noun phrase.

OBJECTIVES
- use an introduction to understand the general theme of a text
- read for related information in stages
- read to complete a table and draw a graph

_____

_____ **?**

Everyone wonders about this from time to time, but there is no answer for each individual person. However, the World Health Organization (WHO) has figures for average life expectancy from the earliest times.

Thousands of years ago, in pre-history, there were many dangers and people only lived for about 20 years. The Ancient Egyptians, in around 3000 BCE, had an average life expectancy of 25. Although they knew a lot about medicine, the Ancient Greeks only lived for an extra three years. In around 0 CE, at the time of the Roman Empire, people died at 28 on average.

In the Middle Ages, around 1400 CE, a wider variety of food was available and the average age at death increased to 33. The average continued to rise over the next 200 years. In the Renaissance, at the time of Michelangelo, most people lived until they were 37.

During the Victorian Age, from around 1850 CE, doctors began to save many more children at birth and life expectancy rose to 45.

By the beginning of the 20th century, average life expectancy was 50, but soon it started to rise quickly. The reason was cleaner houses, cleaner water and a better diet. By 1950 CE, the average age of death was 65.

Thanks to further medical advances, particularly the use of antibiotics, life expectancy continued to rise. At the start of the 21st century, it was 79.

What about the future? Life expectancy is still rising, but not as quickly as in the 20th century. By 2050 CE, scientists predict that it will be 85, but it will take another 500 years to get to the magic age of 100.

Table 1: *Life expectancy through the ages*

Period	Year	Average
pre-history	5000 BCE	20
Ancient Egypt	3000 BCE	
Ancient Greece	1000 BCE	
the Roman Empire	0 CE	
the Middle Ages	1400 CE	
the Renaissance	1600 CE	
the Victorian Age	1850 CE	
the start of 20th century	1900 CE	
the middle of 20th century	1950 CE	
the start of 21st century	2000 CE	
the middle of 21st century	2050 CE	

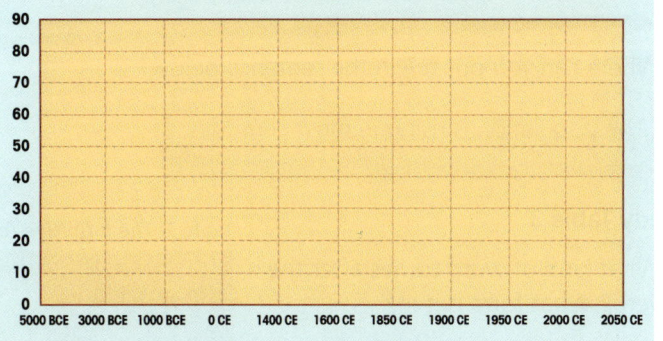

Figure 1: *Life expectancy through the ages*

Lesson 5: Writing and Grammar

A **Look at Table 1.**

1 Write the correct verb form in each space.

2 Complete the sentence below about babies in your country. Circle the correct option.

_____

in hospital / at home.

Table 1: Be born

Most babies	_____		at home.
I / He / She	_____	born	in 1984.
You / We / They	_____		in London.

3 Match the people with the phrases.

a.	Barack Obama		Christmas Day
b.	Charles Darwin and Abraham Lincoln		Australia
c.	Sir Isaac Newton		the same day in 1809
d.	Nicole Kidman and Russell Crowe		Hawaii

4 Write each piece of information in A3 as a full sentence.

5 Write three more interesting sentences about the date or place of birth of famous people.

B **Think again about birth rates and death rates.**

1 What is happening to the population of Europe, Africa and the United States?

2 Look at Table 2. Why do we use the present continuous in this situation? Tick (✓) the correct function below.

Table 2: *Present continuous*

The population	of Europe	is	falling	slightly.
	of Africa		rising	quickly.
People	in the US	are	living	longer.

a.	to say what is happening at the exact moment	☐
b.	to talk about changes happening around the time	☐

3 Read about the birth rate in Italy. Then do some research about the birth rate in your country. Write a similar paragraph about your country.

> The population of Italy is growing very slowly. In 1986, the population was 56.5 million and now it is 58.8 million. That is a growth of only 3.9%. The growth rate for all of Western Europe in that time was 12.4%. The birth rate now is 9.18 births per 1,000 people. The population is growing older too. Twenty-one point six per cent of Italians are over the age of 65.

4 Where can you put *still* in the sentence below?

The population is rising in most countries.

C **Study Table 3.**

1 What kind of word comes after the verb? What form is it in?

Table 3: *The infinitive following a verb*

Life expectancy	started		thousands of years ago.
	continued		in the 20th century.

OBJECTIVES	• use *is / are / was / were born*	• use present continuous to describe change
	• punctuate sentences with a *when* clause	• write about life event customs

2 Study the sentence below. Then write the information in a–c as full sentences in the same way.

> Life expectancy started to rise in around 3000 BCE, and it is still rising.

   a. The population of India / start / rise / 60 years ago, and …
   b. The child death rate / UK / start / fall / 1900s, and …
   c. Internet use / start / increase / end / the last century, and …

D Think about birth, marriage and death customs again.

  1 Write the four parts of the sentence below in the correct order. Then put in the correct punctuation.

   give them presents / someone has a birthday / people / when

  2 Look at Table 4.

  3 Read the text about customs in the UK. Make notes in Figure 1.

  4 Make notes about your culture in Figure 1.

  5 Cover the text about customs in the UK. Write about customs in your country.

Table 4: *Sentences with a* when *cause*

When	a child	has	a birthday,	people buy presents.
When	someone	dies,	the family	buys a stone.

	UK	My culture
Birth		
Marriage		
Death		

Figure 1: *Life events – special customs*

CUSTOMS FOR LIFE EVENTS
There are three important life events in most cultures. There are special customs for each event in UK culture.

Birth When someone has a birthday, people give them presents. A child's present is often a toy, but some people give the child money. They often sing *Happy Birthday to You* at a birthday party.

Marriage When a man and a woman marry, the man gives the woman a ring. He puts it on the third finger of the woman's left hand.

Death When someone dies, the person's family sometimes buys a stone. On the stone, they put the person's name, the date of birth and the date of death. They sometimes put a sentence about the person.

Lesson 6: Writing and Grammar

A Follow the steps.

1 Complete the questions with the correct question word.
   a. _____ did this custom start? / It started at the time of the Aztecs.
   b. _____ did Steve and Liz go on honeymoon? / They went to Florida.
   c. _____ did you buy Tim for his birthday? / I bought him an iPod.
   d. _____ did they travel to the wedding? / They took the train.
   e. _____ did Sue leave the party early? / She was tired.

2 Look at Table 1 and check.

3 Put the words in the correct order to make questions.
   a. Sally / dress / where / her / did / wedding / buy
   b. did / the / how / Year / the / celebrate / New / Romans
   c. party / Martin / at / did / arrive / when / the

4 Use the information to write full questions.
   a. why / life expectancy / start / rise / Middle Ages?
   b. what / the Egyptians / do / when / child / born?

5 Study the example. Write three more questions to ask a partner.

Example: *What did you have for dinner last night?*

Table 1: *Past question forms*

When		this custom	start?	
Where		Steve and Liz	go	on honeymoon?
What	did	you	buy	Tim for his birthday?
How		they	travel	to the wedding?
Why		Sue	leave	the party early?

B Follow the steps.

1 Choose the correct sentence out of i, ii and iii for a and b.

	i	ii	iii
a.	What happens at a christening?	What happen at a christening?	What does happen at a christening?
b.	What happen in 1939?	What did happen in 1939?	What happened in 1939?

2 Ask and answer the questions below in pairs.
   a. What happened in 1945?
   b. What happened in 1969?
   c. What happened in September 2001?

3 Write two more similar questions to ask a partner. You must know the answer!

OBJECTIVES
- practise past question forms
- use patterns with two objects
- practise questions with *happen*

C **Study Tables 2a and 2b.**

Cover the tables and tick (✓) the correct sentences below.

1. My father bought my brother a car. ☐
2. My father bought for my brother a car. ☐
3. My father bought a car for my brother. ☐
4. My father bought a car my brother. ☐

Table 2a: *Sentences with two objects (1)*

S	V	O1 = person	O2 = thing
The guest	gave	the woman	a present.
He		her	

Table 2b: *Sentences with two objects (2)*

S	V	O1 = thing	Prep	O2 = person
The guest	gave	a present	to	the woman.
He		it		her.

D **Think again about events, ceremonies and customs.**

1. Read an e-mail from a Spanish student to a friend in the USA.

From: Carmen@e-mail.com
To: Daisy@e-mail.com
Subject: Las Fallas

Hi Daisy,

I know you want to come to Spain. Next month is the best time. There's a big festival in my city called Las Fallas. People make figures and burn them on fires in the street. There are parades and people dress up in fantastic costumes. There are firework displays every day for a week. It's crazy! You will love it!

Hope to see you soon,
Carmen

2. Write a similar e-mail to a friend about a festival or ceremony in your country.

E **Read the sentences. Circle the correct word or phrase in each case.**

1	The population of Europe	falls / *is falling*	because the death rate is higher than the birth rate.
2	Life expectancy started	rise / to rise	thousands of years ago.
3	The average age of death	still is / is still	rising.
4	How	did you come / came you	to the party?
5	What	did happen / happened	last night?
6	The man is giving	to the baby / the baby	a present.
7	When	a person dies, / dies a person,	people buy flowers.

English Skills for University 2b, Course Book, Unit 1

Grade your progress (1 = poor to 5 = very good)

At the end of Unit 1, I can:

- [ ] listen to a lecture and identify statistics
- [ ] role-play a tutorial about customs in my country
- [ ] use punctuation to understand a written text
- [ ] write about customs in my own country
- [ ] pronounce vowel sounds accurately
- [ ] pronounce c before different vowels
- [ ] use the grammar of the unit accurately

Transfer

Research life expectancy throughout the 20th century in your own country.

Reflect

Think about how tenses were used in this unit. Are they used in the same way in your own language? If not, how are they different?

Unit 2
They Made Our World

Key vocabulary

accident *(n)*
aeroplane *(n)*
airport *(n)*
bicycle *(n)*
bus *(n)*
comfortable *(adj)*
convenient *(adj)*
car *(n)*
crash *(n/v)*
cyclist *(n)*
dangerous *(adj)*
death *(n)*
economical *(adj)*
expensive *(adj)*
fast *(adj)*
fly *(v)*
inconvenient *(adj)*

involve *(v)*
journey *(n)*
measure *(v)*
method of transport *(n)*
motorbike *(n)*
motorist *(n)*
passenger *(n)*
pedestrian *(n)*
safe *(adj)*
safety *(n)*
slow *(adj)*
statement *(n)*
traffic *(n)*
train *(n)*
uncomfortable *(adj)*
witness *(n)*

Unit 2 They Made Our World

Lesson 1: Listening

A Look at the pictures. What do they have in common?

B Compare methods of transport.

> I think riding a motorbike is more dangerous than driving a car.

C Look at Table 1 opposite.

1 Number the methods in order. If you think cars had the most accidents, put *1* next to the car.

2 🔊 **1:20** Listen. Predict the next word. Then complete the *Accidents p.a.* and *Order* columns.

3 Was the order of methods similar to your predictions?

D 🔊 **1:21 Listen to part of the talk again.**

1 What two questions does the speaker ask?

2 The speaker says: *One way is to look at the number of accidents for each method.* What does this sentence tell you about later information in the talk?

3 Read the Skills Check and check.

Skills Check

Predicting the structure of a talk

- Speakers sometimes help us to predict the structure of a talk.
  Examples:

The speaker	
says:	**will say later:**
How can we measure safety? **One way** is …	**Another way** is … OR **The other way** is … OR **The best way** is …
We **could** look at …	Alternatively, we **could** look at …

OBJECTIVES
- predict the structure of a talk
- hear and record large numbers
- listen to take notes

Table 1: *Transport safety in the US*

Method	Accidents p.a.	Order	Death p.a.	Death p. billion km	Chance of dying on method of transport: 1 in …
🚲					
🚢					
🚌					
🚗					
🏍					
🚶					
✈					
🚄					

Source: *US Department of Transport, 2002*

E Think about other ways of measuring transport safety.

1 Look at the other column headings in the table. What do you think they mean?

2 Write a short explanation of each heading.

Accidents p.a.
the number of *accidents each year for each method of transport*

Deaths p.a.
the number of _____

Deaths p. billion km
the number of _____

Chance of dying on method of transport
the chances of dying _____

3 🔊 **1:22** Listen and check your ideas.

F Work in groups of eight.

1 Each person must choose one method of transport.

2 🔊 **1:23** Listen for information about your method. Complete the remaining three columns in Table 1.

3 Ask and answer other students in your group about the figures for each method of transport.

English Skills for University 2b, Course Book, Unit 2

Lesson 2: Speaking

A Look at the picture. Answer the questions below.

1 What is happening?
2 When there is a road accident, what do:
- the drivers do?
- the police do?
- any witnesses do?

B 1:24 Listen to two conversations.

1 Match Conversations 1 and 2 with illustrations A and B.
2 Explain what happened.

C Look at the conversations. Think of a verb for each space.

Conversation 1
P: So, what happened?
C: I <u>was riding</u> my bike along this road. The door of a car suddenly _____ and I hit it. I _____ off my bike.
P: Are you all right?
C: I hurt my arm, but I don't think it's broken.
D: I'm so sorry. I _____ about my appointment. I was late, you see.
P: Late?
D: Yes, I was late to see the doctor. I _____ in the mirror before I opened the door.

Conversation 2
P: So, what happened?
D1: I _____ at the red light. The car behind _____. He went into the back of my car.
D2: I'm sorry. I was …
P: _____ you _____ on your cellphone?
D2: No, I was …
D1: Yes, he was. He _____ on his phone and he _____ the red light.
P: Is that true?
D2: Well, yes. I was talking on my phone, but I _____ at the road too.
P: So, why did you hit the car in front then?

24 English Skills for University 2b, Course Book, Unit 2

| OBJECTIVES | • describe an accident | • contrast past forms in narrative |

D **1:25 Listen to Conversation 1 again.**

1 Complete it with verbs in the correct form.

2 Find two different past verb forms. Why are they used?

3 Read Skills Check 1.

E **Look at Conversation 2.**

1 Complete it with the correct form of the verbs below.

| talk   stop   look   not see   not stop |

2 **1:26** Listen and check.

F **Work in groups of three.**

1 **1:27** Listen to both conversations again.

2 Practise each conversation three times. Play each role once.

3 Invent a similar situation. Write a conversation for three speakers.

4 Role-play your conversation.

G **Work in pairs.**

1 Think of a similar situation from your life.
- Plan what you want to say and make notes.
- Look up in a dictionary or ask your teacher about any key words you need.

2 Take it in turns. Describe the accident.
- Use the correct past tenses.
- Ask questions about your partner's accident.

Skills Check 1

Interrupted actions

- Actions are sometimes interrupted.

action   interruption   result

Examples:

Action	Interruption	Result
I **was riding** my bike.	The door of a car suddenly **opened**.	I **hit** it. I **fell** off my bike.
I **was thinking** about my appointments.	I **didn't look** in the mirror.	

past continuous   past simple   past simple

Skills Check 2

Improving your pronunciation

- When you learn a new word, say it three times.
- Think: *Which sounds are difficult for me?* Practise those sounds.
- Think: *Where is the stress?* Practise saying the word with the correct stress.
- Say the word ten more times.

English Skills for University 2b, Course Book, Unit 2

Lesson 3: Vocabulary and Pronunciation

A **Study the adjectives in the green box.**

1 Match opposites.

2 Use the adjectives to talk about methods of transport.

Example: *Riding a bicycle is economical.*

> fast   convenient   safe
> comfortable   uncomfortable
> inconvenient   expensive
> dangerous   slow   economical

B **Complete each series in the table with a word from the box below.**

> drive   land   check-in   middle lane   ride

1	take off	fly	
2	get in		stop/get out
3	get on		get off
4	slow lane		fast lane
5		departure lounge	boarding gate

C **Copy the table below in your notebook. Add the words in the blue box to the appropriate column.**

- You can use some words more than once.
- You can write more than one word in a column.

Transport	Person	Place	Related verbs
bus	driver	bus station	drive

> airport   ride   port   bicycle
> drive   captain   sail   plane
> ship   fly   harbour   train
> cyclist   driver   railway station
> pilot   cycle lane

D **Read Skills Check 1. Choose three new words from this unit. Write entries in your vocabulary notebook for each word.**

Skills Check 1

Organizing your vocabulary

- Here is one way to organize your vocabulary notebook.
  - Mark stress and silent letters.
  - Draw pictures, use symbols.

Words	Opposites	Series
take 'off (v)	land	take 'off - fly - land

Same set: plane (n) 'airport (n) 'pilot (n)

OBJECTIVES
- revise and develop vocabulary related to transport
- practise pronunciation – word stress patterns
- organize and record vocabulary
- start a conversation

E Tick (✓) the stress pattern for each word. Then look at the Skills Check.

		Oo	oO	Ooo	oOo
1	accident			✓	
2	airport				
3	appointment				
4	arrive				
5	bicycle				
6	comfortable				
7	dangerous				
8	depart				
9	departure				
10	expensive				
11	involve				
12	passenger				
13	pilot				
14	police				
15	station				
16	traffic				

Skills Check 2

Stressing long words

- Most nouns and adjectives with two syllables have the stress on the first syllable.
  Examples:
  'traffic   'airport   'happy

- But many two-syllable verbs have the stress on the second syllable.
  Examples:
  arr'ive   de'part

- Three-syllable words are usually stressed on the first or second syllable.
  Examples:
  'passenger   ex'pensive

- People often recognize a word from the stressed sound only.

F We often start a conversation by talking about a journey.

1. 1:28 Listen to two conversations. Answer the questions.
   a. How did each speaker travel?
   b. What was the journey like?

2. 1:29 Listen again and complete the conversations.

3. Practise the conversations in pairs.

4. Work in pairs.
   Student 1: You have travelled to see Student 2. How did you travel? What was the journey like?
   Student 2: Student 1 has travelled to see you. Start a conversation about the journey.
   Swap roles.

Conversation 1
A: Did you _____ here?
B: Yes, I did.
A: What was the _____ like?
B: It was _____!
A: Oh dear!

Conversation 2
A: How did you _____ here?
B: I came by _____.
A: How was the _____?
B: _____.
A: Oh, good.

Lesson 4: Reading

A **Study Table 1.**

1 Which came first? Number the methods of transport in order. (The oldest = 1.)

2 When, approximately, did people start using each method? Think of a date.

B **Scan the text opposite.**

1 Find and underline eight names in 30 seconds. What is each name?

2 Find and circle eight numbers in 20 seconds. What is each number?

C **Prepare to read the text opposite.**

1 Read the heading. Answer the question.

2 Read the introduction. What is the text about?

3 What order will the information be in? Why?

4 Check with the subheadings and illustrations.

D **Work in groups of four.**

1 Choose one method of transport each. Find the key information and write it in Table 1.

2 Cover the text. Ask the other students in your group about the other methods. Complete the table.

E **Read the Skills Check.**

F **Explain the words below to the other students in your group in Exercise D.**

> member   inquest   wheel
> propeller   survived

G **Find and highlight examples of the past simple and past continuous in the text.**

Skills Check

Guessing words from context

- You will often read new words in a text. You cannot guess the meaning of a single word, but the word is in a phrase, a sentence and a paragraph.

Examples:

Word	Context
steam	a **steam** car
steep	down a **steep** hill
flight	He made the first **flight** … The plane, called …
competition	There was a **competition** between different engines. Many people came to watch.

Table 1: *The first deaths in travel accidents*

Method	Date	Location	Person	Car/Plane, etc.	Driver/Pilot, etc.
planes					
pedestrians					
cars					
trains					

OBJECTIVES
• predict the order of information in a text
• understand new words in context
• understand past verb forms in context

WHEN IS IT BAD TO BE 1ST?

There are thousands of accidents every day involving trains, pedestrians, cars and planes. In many of these accidents, people die. But when did the first person die in a train accident, a car accident or a plane crash?

Trains
On 15th September, 1830, there was a competition in Liverpool, England, between different railway engines. Many people came to watch, including William Huskisson, a member of the British Government. Huskisson was talking and did not see one of the engines. It was called the *Rocket* and it was travelling at about 40 kilometres per hour. It hit him and he became the first person to die in a railway accident.

Pedestrians
A scientist called Mary Ward was the first pedestrian to die in a road accident. On 31st August, 1869, she fell under a steam car in Ireland. A woman called Bridget Driscoll was the first person to die in an accident involving a petrol car. She was crossing a road in a London park in 1896. A man called Arthur Edsall hit her. He was driving at only six kilometres per hour. The lawyer at the inquest into Bridget's death said, 'This kind of accident must never happen again.'

Cars
On 25th February, 1899, Edwin Sewell, an engineer, was driving his car down a steep hill near London. One wheel broke and he hit a wall. Sewell became the first driver to die in a road accident. His passenger, a soldier called Richer, fell out of the car and died three days later in hospital.

Planes
Orville Wright was a maker of bicycles, but he was famous because he made the first flight on 17th December, 1903, in the USA. The plane, called *Flyer 1*, travelled 37 metres. Five years later, Thomas Selfridge, an American soldier, took off with Orville in the same plane. They were flying at about 25 metres and the propeller broke. The plane crashed and Selfridge became the first person to die in a plane accident. Orville broke his leg, but he survived the accident.

English Skills for University 2b, Course Book, Unit 2

Lesson 5: Writing and Grammar

A **Look at Table 1.**

1 Complete it with the correct verb form in each space.

Table 1: *Past continuous*

I / He / She / It	_____	riding.
You / We / They	_____	

2 Match the past continuous actions with the past simple interruptions and results.

a.	Jim was riding his horse.	He didn't see his station and went past it.
b.	Tina and Liz were driving home.	She slipped and fell in the river.
c.	Sally was getting on the boat.	A friend saw them and took them home in his car.
d.	Stan was reading a book.	A dog ran in the road and they hit it.
e.	Tom and Grace were waiting for a taxi.	He fell off and broke his arm.

3 Look at the *Planes* paragraph on page 29 again.
   a. What action was happening before the accident?
   b. What was the interruption?
   c. What was the result?

B **Link actions together.**

1 Write the two sentences below as one sentence. What word do you need to join them?

Sally was getting on the boat. She slipped and fell in the river.

Sally _____.

2 Write the sentence below in another way. Use the adverb from the sentence and add a comma.

Jim fell off his horse and broke his arm.

_____ Jim _____.

3 Read the Skills Check and check.

Skills Check

Using *when* with interrupted actions

- We can write the **action** and **interruption** in the same sentence.
  Examples:

Action		Interruption
The *Rocket* **was travelling** at about 40 kph	when	it **hit** William Huskisson.
He **was driving** down a steep hill		a wheel **broke.**

- We can also write the **interruption** and **result** in the same sentence.
  Examples:

	Interruption		Result
When	the wheel **broke**	,	Sewell **hit** a wall.
	the plane **crashed**		Orville **broke** his leg.

OBJECTIVES
- use past continuous
- write a report of an accident
- link past tenses with *when*

C **Study Table 2. Complete the two patterns.**

- past continuous + *when* + _____
- *When* + _____ + _____

Table 2: *Linking past forms with* **when**

| The car | was | travelling | at 80 kph … |

| … when | a wheel | broke. |

| When | the wheel | broke, | the car | hit | a wall. |

D **Work in pairs.**

1 Study the text from your teacher. Look carefully at the grammar.

2 Tell your partner about it. Use Table 3 to help you. Then swap roles.

Table 3: *The worst air and sea disasters*

	Air disaster	Sea disaster
Date	27/03/1977	30/01/1945
Place	Tenerife (w. coast Af.)	Baltic Sea (nr coast Ger.)
Name	2 x 747 planes	Wilhelm Gustloff
Action	1 = taking off	Danzig ➡ Kiel
Interruption	hit 1 on ground	torpedo hit ship
Result	583 d.	>7,000 d.

E **Read the witness statement from one of the accidents in Lesson 2.**

1 Put the verbs in brackets into the correct form (past simple or past continuous).

> I _____ (stand) at the bus stop in Blatchington Road when I _____ (see) the accident. Some cars _____ (wait) at the traffic lights about 35 metres from me. The lights were red, but one car _____ (not stop). The driver _____ (go) into the back of the car in front. I think he _____ (talk) on his cellphone and _____ (not look) at the road. When he _____ (hit) the car in front, there was a terrible bang.

2 Write a similar report of an accident you saw or were involved in.

Lesson 6: Writing and Grammar

A Read about the Hindenburg. Write notes in the table.

The most famous air accident in history involved the *Hindenburg* airship. The *Hindenburg* was the largest flying machine in history. It took off from Frankfurt Airport. It was going to New Jersey. There were 36 passengers and 61 crew members. It was landing in New Jersey on May 3rd, 1937, when a fire started. When the airship fell to the ground, 13 passengers and 22 crew died.

| | Accidents ||
	Hindenburg	Titanic
From		Southampton
To		New York
Pass./Crew		1,316/913
Action		sailing N. At. (14/04/1912)
Interruption		hit iceberg
Result		sank
Pass./Crew dead		818/698

B Read the notes about the *Titanic*. Write a paragraph.

C Complete the sentences below so that they are true for you.

1 I was coming to the university yesterday when _____.

2 When I arrived in class yesterday morning, _____.

3 Last week, I was having lunch when _____.

4 When classes finished yesterday, _____.

32 English Skills for University 2b, Course Book, Unit 2

OBJECTIVES
- write about an historic transport accident
- conduct and write about a survey

D **Look at the bar graph.**

1 Complete the report with the words in the box.

| two   one   three   six   half   five |

There are 32 students in my class and they come to university by six different methods. Nearly _____ the students come by bus. _____ students live very close and always walk. _____ students usually ride their bikes, though two of them sometimes walk. _____ students live outside the city and come by train. They walk from the station. _____ students come to university on their mopeds (small motorbikes) and _____ drives.

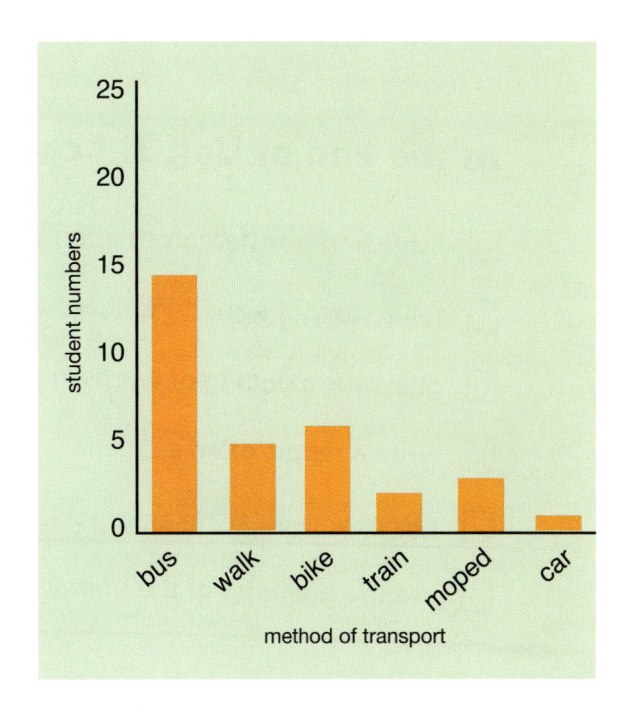

2 Conduct a survey of students in your class.
- Ask how they travel to university.
- Record answers, make notes and draw a bar graph.
- Write a report.

E **Read the sentences. Circle the correct word or phrase in each case.**

1	A way / One way	to measure safety	is to look at accidents for each method of travel.
2	There are two roads.	Shall we take this one or	another one? / the other one?
3	Alternatively,	we must / we could	go by train.
4	How / What	was the traffic like	on the way here?
5	The car	travelled / was travelling	at 80 kph …
6	… when it	hit / was hitting	the wall.
7	When the plane	was crashing, / crashed,	the pilot died.

Grade your progress (1 = poor to 5 = very good)

At the end of Unit 2, I can:

- [ ] listen and transfer information to a table
- [ ] tell a story of something that happened to me
- [ ] guess the meaning of words in context
- [ ] write a report of an accident
- [ ] record vocabulary in an organized way
- [ ] use the grammar of the unit accurately

Transfer

Think about an interesting event that happened when you were young. Make notes and then explain what happened to a classmate.

Reflect

Think about how often you begin stories by setting the scene. Try to apply this as often as you can to potential stories and events that happen to you.

Unit 3
Media and Literature

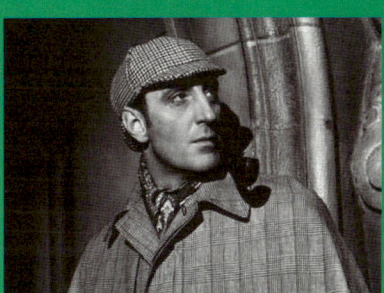

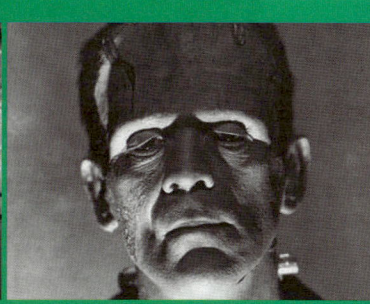

Key vocabulary

action film (n)
actor (n)
actress (n)
adventure (n)
author (n)
autobiography (n)
cartoon (n)
character (n)
comedy (n)
crime (n)
crime film (n)
direct (a film) (v)
director (n)
drama (n)
favourite (adj)
historical film (n)

horror film (n)
love story (n)
novel (n)
play (a part/role) (v)
role (n)
scene (n)
science fiction (sci-fi) film (n)
set (be set in) (v)

Unit 3 Media and Literature

Lesson 1: Listening

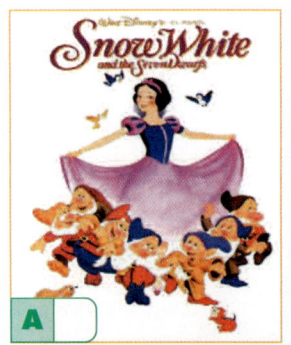

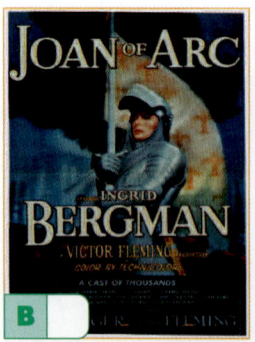

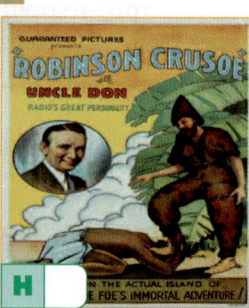

A Look at the old film posters.

1 Match the story types in the green box with the posters.

2 1:30 Listen and match each extract with one of the posters.

3 Did you understand the key words and phrases in the blue box in context?

> comedy   cartoon   love story
> science fiction   crime   historical
> horror   adventure

> mystery   make you jump   set (v)
> character   laugh

B Look at Table 1 below and Figure 1 opposite.

1 What information do you expect to hear?

2 1:31 Listen to a research report. Predict the next word. Then complete Table 1.

3 Complete Figure 1 opposite.

Table 1: *Bestsellers in English in paperbacks (2002)*

Book type	Total
(Pirates)	
(The Life of Lord Nelson)	
(My Life in Cinema)	
(A History of Comedy)	

Book type	Total
(Crime)	
(Henry VIII)	
(Horror)	
(Love Story)	

Book type	Total
(Sci-Fi)	
other	

36   English Skills for University 2b, Course Book, Unit 3

OBJECTIVES	• listen to a research report • listen to complete tables and charts	• listen to hear statistics • listen for examples and lists

C Listen to the introduction to some research.

1. 🔊 **1:32** Listen. Make notes in your notebook under the following headings: *Date*, *Name and country*, *Number*, *Age*, *Tasks 1 and 2*.

2. 🔊 **1:33** Listen. Which word in the tables below does the speaker explain? What is the explanation?

3. Look at the tables. What do you expect to hear?

D You are going to hear the results of the research.

1. 🔊 **1:34** Listen and complete Table 1.

2. 🔊 **1:35** Listen and complete Table 2 or Table 3.

3. Tell other students the results for your group of people.

E What about you?

1. What's your favourite type of film?

2. What's your favourite type of book?

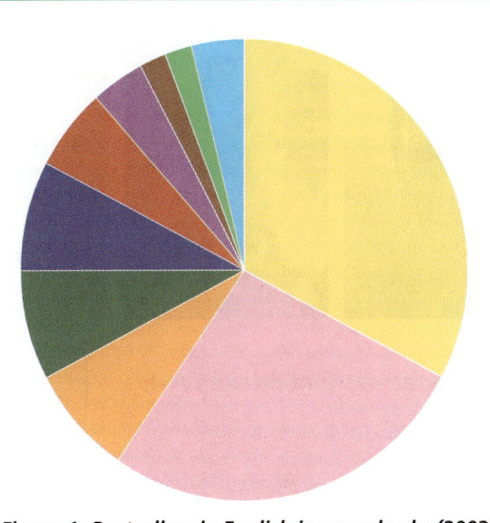

Figure 1: *Bestsellers in English in paperbacks (2002)*
Source of raw material: *Guardian Unlimited*

Table 1: *Film types by order of preference*

Type	Order	Type	Order
(sword)		(mask)	
(POW)		(ghost)	
(boy)		(heart)	
(gun)		(rocket)	

Table 2: *Favourite types of film – females*

Type	%	Type	%
(sword)		(mask)	
(POW)		(ghost)	
(boy)		(heart)	
(gun)		(rocket)	
		other	11

Table 3: *Favourite types of film – males*

Type	%	Type	%
(sword)		(mask)	
(POW)		(ghost)	
(boy)		(heart)	
(gun)		(rocket)	
		other	4

Skills Check

Examples and lists

- Speakers often use a word or phrase, then give an example.
  Example:
  He used **traditional categories** for film types – **Love story**, **Science fiction**, **Crime**, etc.
- If there are many examples, speakers end the list with **etc.** (*etcetera*) or **and so on.**
- If you do not understand a word or phrase, wait for the example(s).
- If the list ends with *etc.* or *and so on*, think of more examples.

English Skills for University 2b, Course Book, Unit 3

Lesson 2: Speaking

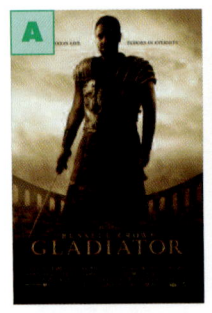

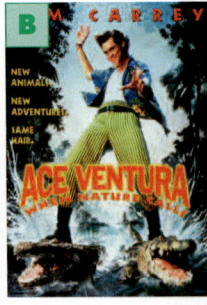

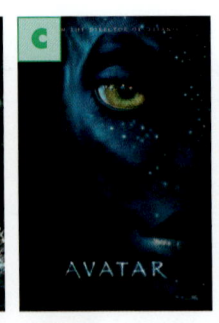

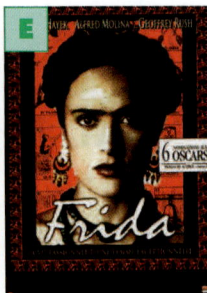

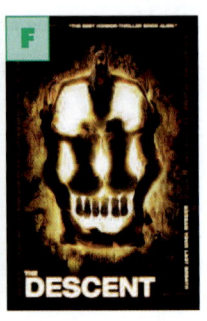

A Look at the film posters A–F.

1 Name the types of film.
2 What do you know about each film?

> Salma Hayek plays the part of Frida Kahlo.

> I saw it a few years ago. It's really good.

B 🔊 1:36 Listen to a conversation. Which film are they talking about?

C Look at the conversation.

1 Can you remember the questions?
2 🔊 1:37 Listen again and check. Write the questions into the spaces.
3 🔊 1:38 Listen again. Then practise the conversation in pairs.

D Think about fact and possibility.

1 Why do the speakers use *probably*, *perhaps* and *I guess* in the conversation?
2 Read the Skills Check.

E Work in pairs. Talk about your favourite film.

1 Choose a film. Plan what you want to say. Answer the questions in Exercise C1.
2 Have a conversation. Ask and answer questions. Swap roles.

A: So, _____?
B: Mm, I think it's probably _____.
A: _____?
B: Well, it's a historical drama, but I guess it's an action film too.
A: _____?
B: It's set in Roman times. A soldier becomes a slave. Then he becomes a _____. He becomes the greatest _____ because he's so brave.
A: _____?
B: The main character's Russell Crowe.
A: Oh, really. I like him. _____?
B: I'm not going to tell you. Watch it!
A: Perhaps I will.

Skills Check

Recognize fact and possibility

- We give facts with the present simple. We can change facts into possibilities with *perhaps* or *probably*.

Fact:
It's set in Roman times.
The main character**'s** Russell Crowe.

Possibility:
It's **probably** *Gladiator*.
Perhaps I will (watch it).

---

38 English Skills for University 2b, Course Book, Unit 3

OBJECTIVES
- talk about favourite films
- conduct a survey
- distinguish between fact and possibility

Table 1: *Story type preference – results*

Story type	S1	S2	S3	S4	S5	S6	S7	S8	S9	S10	Total	Rank	% = 1
🔫													
❤️													
🚀													
👦													
👑👑													
👻													
🗡️													

F Look at the college handout.
  1 Read it carefully. Then cover it.
  2 Explain the process to a partner.

G Follow the instructions in the college handout. Use some of this language.
  - Could you put these story types in order of preference?
  - What's your favourite type?
  - What's second?
  - And next?
  - OK. Number 4?
  - Fifth place?
  - Sixth?
  - And in last place?
  - So that's Crime first, Horror second …

Table 2: *Favourite types of story*

Story type	Order
Crime	
Love	
Sci-fi	
Comedy	
Historical	
Horror	
Adventure	

Greenhill College
A SURVEY

Do a survey of people in your class or group. Find out their favourite types of story in a film or novel. Put your results in a table and a pie chart.

1. Look at the list of story types in Table 1.
2. Speak to everybody in your class or group. Ask them to put the story types in order of preference (*1* = favourite type). Write their answers in Table 1.
3. Calculate the total for each student.
4. Calculate the order (lowest number is one, same number is =).
5. Calculate the percentage for favourite type (e.g., if 2 people out of 5 say Crime = *1*, percentage is 40%).
6. Compare your results with the other people in your class or group. They should be the same!
7. Complete Table 2.
8. Complete Figure 1. Label it.

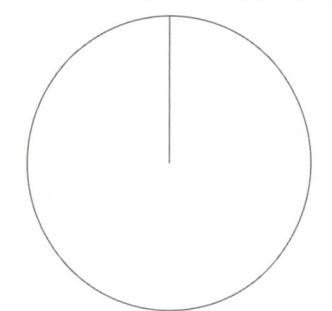

Figure 1: *Favourite types of story*

English Skills for University 2b, Course Book, Unit 3

Lesson 3: Vocabulary and Pronunciation

A **Work in teams. Look at the film and book quiz.**

1 Study the underlined words.
2 Answer the questions. (1 mark for each correct answer [total 9])
3 Which team knows the most?

1. Who is the film <u>director</u> in picture A?
2. Who <u>directed</u> the films *Psycho, The Birds* and *Rear Window*?
3. What is the name of the <u>character</u> in picture B?
4. Who wrote the <u>novels</u> *The House of the Spirits* and *City of the Beasts*?
5. Which country were the <u>authors</u> Tolstoy and Dostoyevsky from?
6. Which <u>actress</u> played the <u>role</u> of Maria Elena in *Vicky Cristina Barcelona*?
7. Whose <u>autobiography</u> is called *The Greatest*?
8. Who is the <u>actor</u> in picture C?

B **Study the pairs of sentences below.**

1 🔊 1:39 Listen. What do the underlined words have in common?

a. It's a fantastic film. Go and <u>see</u> it.
   I went swimming in the <u>sea</u> last week.

b. Kim Basinger played the <u>role</u> of Eminem's mother in *8 mile*.
   I had a cheese <u>roll</u> for lunch.

2 Read Skills Check 1 and check.
3 Add homophones to the table.

meat	meet	where	
write		made	
sun		by	
no		sail	

Skills Check 1

Homophones
- Sometimes two words in English have the same sound, but different spelling.
  Examples:
  sea – see
  role – roll
  meat – meet
- Make sure you know the correct spelling for each meaning.

40 English Skills for University 2b, Course Book, Unit 3

OBJECTIVES	• revise and develop vocabulary related to films and books • learn homophones
	• learn about group words

C Study the words.

film		lawyer
meat		Mars
colour		autumn
sport		bakers
job		comedy
season		juice
planet		yellow
shop		June
month		football
drink		chicken

Skills Check 2

Group words

- The word *colour* is a group word. There are many words in the group, e.g., *yellow*, *green*, *blue*, *red*, *white*, *black*.
- The word *season* is also a group word. There are only a few words in the group, e.g., *spring*, *summer*, *autumn* and *winter*.
- Learn group words. They are very useful. If you do not know the exact word, you can use the group word.

Examples:
It's a colour. It's red and yellow.
It's a kind of shop. It sells houses.

1 Find pairs of words.
2 Explain the relationship.
3 Read Skills Check 2 and check.

D Look at the word sets below.

1 Choose one set. Write words for the word set.
2 Compare your lists. Find people with the same word set. Add more words to the list.

PARTS OF THE BODY
hand

FURNITURE
chair

BUILDINGS
church

MOTOR VEHICLES
car

RELATIONS
sister

DISEASES
cancer

CLOTHES
shirt

SCHOOL SUBJECTS
Maths

Lesson 4: Reading

A **Prepare to read the text opposite.**
1. Read the heading. Can you answer the question?
2. Read the introduction. What is the text about?
3. What order will the information be in? Why? Check with the illustrations.

B **Scan the text.**
1. Find the names of two authors.
2. Find two book titles.
3. Find the names of two story characters.
4. Read the Skills Check.

C **Work in groups of five.**
1. Choose one type of novel each. Find the key information and write it in Table 1.
2. Ask and answer about the other types of novel.

D **Read your text again.**
1. Identify the summary of the story.
2. Learn the summary. Check the meaning of new words.
3. In your group, give the summary. Explain new words.

E **Which of the five novels would you like to read? Why?**

Skills Check

Identifying titles and characters
- Titles in texts in English are often in *italics* or in 'quotation marks'.
  Examples: *Frankenstein*   'The Time Machine'
- We use capital letters for nouns, verbs, pronouns and adjectives in titles.
- We print the names of real people and characters in novels the same way.
  Examples:

Real people	People in novels
Mark Twain was born in 1835.	A poor boy called **Tom Sawyer** …
Mary Shelley died in 1851.	A scientist called **Dr Frankenstein** …

Table 1: *Writers and their famous novels*

Type	Writer	Born	Died	Novel title	Date	Main person
Love						
Crime						
Horror						
Sci-fi						
Adventure						

OBJECTIVES
- understand specific information
- understand summaries of stories
- recognize names and titles in a text

Who wrote the most famous stories in English Literature?

Do you like love stories? What about horror stories, crime novels or science fiction? Or do you prefer a good adventure novel? Read about the most famous novel in your favourite genre.

1 The most famous love story in English literature is probably 'Pride and Prejudice' by Jane Austen. She was born in the south of England in 1775 and died in 1817, aged 41. She wrote six famous novels, including 'Pride and Prejudice' in 1813. It is set in early 19th-century England. Elizabeth Bennett meets a man called Darcy. She hates him at first, but slowly falls in love with him.

2 The most famous detective in English literature is probably Sherlock Holmes in the short stories by Sir Arthur Conan Doyle. Doyle was born in Edinburgh, Scotland, in 1859 and died in 1930, aged 71. He wrote the Holmes stories between 1887 and 1927. They are set in Victorian England. In each story, something strange happens and Holmes, a private detective, solves a crime.

3 Perhaps the most famous horror story in English literature is *Frankenstein* by Mary Shelley. She was born in London in 1797 and died in 1851, aged 54. She wrote *Frankenstein* in 1818. It is set in the 19th century in Germany, Switzerland and England. A scientist called Dr Frankenstein makes a man from parts of dead people. He brings it to life with electricity. The monster is unhappy and does terrible things.

4 Perhaps the most famous science fiction story in English literature is *The Time Machine* by H. G. Wells. He was born in the south of England in 1866 and died in 1946, aged 79. He wrote *The Time Machine* in 1895. The novel is set in Victorian England. A scientist, called The Time Traveller, makes a machine. It can move a person to any time in the past or the future. The main character has many adventures before he destroys the machine.

5 The most famous adventure story in English literature could be 'The Adventures of Tom Sawyer' by Mark Twain. He was born in the south of the United States in 1835 and died in 1910, aged 74. He wrote 'Tom Sawyer' between 1874 and 1875. It is set in Missouri, Twain's home state, in about 1845. A poor boy called Tom Sawyer has many adventures before he finds a treasure of $12,000 and becomes rich.

Lesson 5: Writing and Grammar

A Look again at the story summaries opposite.

1. Underline the verbs.
2. Which tense is used for a story summary?
3. Read the Skills Check.
4. Write a brief summary of a story you know well. Then compare it with other students' summaries.

B Read and complete the text with the name of the play and the author.

> Perhaps the most famous play in English literature is _____ by _____. He was born in central England in 1564 and died in London in 1616, aged 52. He probably wrote the play in 1597, but nobody is sure. It is a love story set in the 16th century in Italy. _____ are in love, but they cannot be together because their families hate each other. At the end of the play, they both die.

C Look at the boxes.

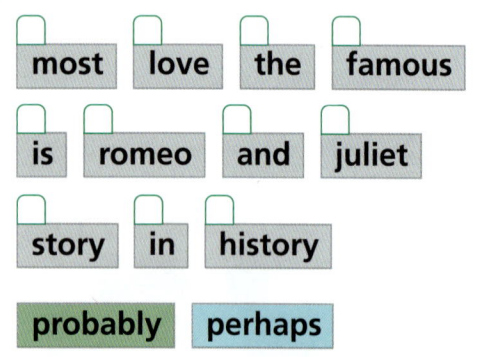

most	love	the	famous
is	romeo	and	juliet
story	in	history

probably   perhaps

1. Number the boxes in order.
2. Where can you put the word in the green box in the sentences?
3. What about the word in the blue box?
4. Write the sentences. Remember punctuation!

D Write a paragraph about the most famous writer in your country and one of his/her stories.

A scientist called Dr Frankenstein makes a man from parts of dead people. He brings it to life with electricity. The monster is unhappy and does terrible things.

The novel is set in Victorian England. A scientist, called The Time Traveller, makes a machine. It can move a person to any time in the past or the future. The main character has many adventures before he destroys the machine.

Skills Check

Summarizing stories

- We use the **present simple** to summarize the story in a book or film. We are not really telling a story – we are saying what happens.
Example:
It's set in Roman times. A soldier **becomes** a slave. Then he **becomes** a gladiator.
Dr Frankenstein **makes** a man from parts of dead people. He **brings** it to life.

OBJECTIVES
- use present simple to summarize a story
- use direct speech
- write about a genre of film

E Read about comedy films. Write notes in the table.

Name	Walt Disney
Born	1901, Chicago, US
Died	1966, Florida, US
Age	65
First film	'Tommy Tucker's Tooth'
Date	1922
Number	>600
Info about films	many have mouse = Mickey; his friends = Minnie (mouse), Pluto (dog), Donald (duck)

COMEDY FILMS

The most famous comedy films in history are probably the ones with Charlie Chaplin. Chaplin was born in 1889 in London. He made his first film, called *Making a Living*, in 1914. He made more than 75 films. He died in Switzerland in 1977, aged 88. In most of his films, Chaplin plays a person with a funny walk, a hat and a stick. He has a lot of trouble, but he always gets the girl.

F Read the notes about cartoon films. Write a paragraph in your notebook.

G Read the typical sentences from love stories.

1 Which are direct speech? How do you know?
2 What is the difference in meaning between the underlined verbs?
3 What is the difference grammatically between *say* and *tell*?

a. Martha was very unhappy. She didn't <u>speak</u> to Henry ever again.

b. Charles and Daphne <u>talked</u> for hours.

c. 'Goodbye, for now,' David <u>said</u>.

d. 'Do you still love me?' Janet <u>asked</u>.

e. 'I don't love you any more,' Margaret <u>told</u> Ralph.

H Read the sentences below.

1 Complete them with a verb from Exercise G.
2 Write the sentences with punctuation in your notebook.

a. I love her with all my heart Simon _____ his friend.

b. Will you marry me Liam _____ Elizabeth.

c. Goodbye Jim Sandra _____ and they never _____ again.

d. Graham is the man for me Sally _____ Barbara. He _____ about things I understand.

English Skills for University 2b, Course Book, Unit 3   45

Lesson 6: Writing and Grammar

A **Read the start of some stories.**

1 What type of story is each one?
2 Find two verb forms. Number them *1* and *2*.
3 How does the writer choose between the two verb forms?
4 Read Skills Check 1 and check.

> **A** Cinderella was doing the housework. She was washing the kitchen floor and cooking lunch at the same time. She was singing to herself. Suddenly, somebody tapped at the door and a letter dropped onto the mat.

> **B** The sun was shining, but there was a large black cloud coming towards the two men. They were climbing fast, but the hill was very steep. Suddenly, the rain started.

> **C** She was running fast, but the creature was getting closer. Her heart was beating faster than ever before. She looked left and right. The walls were high. Suddenly, she saw a door in the wall on the right.

> **D** Jenny was lying on her bed. She was holding her phone in her hand, but it wasn't ringing. She was hoping with all her heart that Paul wasn't angry with her. Suddenly, there was a knock at the door.

> **E** People were having fun in the park. Some were playing ball games and others were flying kites. A few people were rowing boats on the lake. Suddenly, a large shape appeared in the sky. People stopped and looked up.

B **Write the start of a story.**

1 Choose the type of story.
2 Plan how to set the scene and decide what will happen.
3 Write the start of your story.
4 Exchange your texts with other students. Say what type of story each is.

C **Read the first paragraph of a story.**

1 Put the verbs in brackets into the correct form.
2 Listen to your teacher and check your ideas.

> They _____ (fly) at about 50 metres. The pilot _____ (check) the height, then _____ (start) the landing engines. She _____ (speak) to the crew. 'We _____ (land),' she _____ (say). 'Prepare yourselves.' The spaceship _____ (land) softly on the surface of the Moon. The pilot _____ (stop) the engines. 'I _____ (open) the doors now,' she _____ (tell) the crew.

Skills Check 1

Using past tenses in a story

- There are two main past tenses.
  Examples:
  past continuous   She **was reading** a book.
  past simple   She **got** up and **went** out.

- We use the **past continuous** to **set the scene** at the start of the story.
  Examples:
  Cinderella **was doing** the housework.
  She **was washing** the kitchen floor.

- We use the **past simple** for **events** in the story.
  Examples:
  Suddenly, somebody **tapped** at the door.
  A letter **dropped** onto the mat.

---

46   English Skills for University 2b, Course Book, Unit 3

OBJECTIVES	• use past continuous to set the scene	• learn and practise reflexive pronouns
	• revise past tenses and direct speech	• write the start of a story

D Study the sentences in the box.

1 Find the mistakes and correct them.

2 Read Skills Check 2 and check.

3 Cover the Skills Check. Complete Table 1.

4 Cover the Skills Check and Table 1. Write the correct reflexive pronoun in each space.
   a. Do you ever talk to _____?
   b. We painted the house _____.
   c. I hurt _____ playing football.
   d. Sometimes students ask _____, 'How can I do better in this subject?'

- I looked at me in the mirror.
- A: 'Did anyone help Jim?'
  B: 'No, he did all the work him.'
- 'I really do love him,' Emma said to Emma.

Skills Check 2

Reflexive pronouns

- In English, we do not say, ~~I said to me~~. We say, *I said to myself*.
- There is a reflexive (looking back) pronoun for each person.

Subject	Object	Reflexive
I	me	myself
you	you (singular)	yourself
he	him	himself

- Use a reflexive pronoun when S = O.
  Examples:

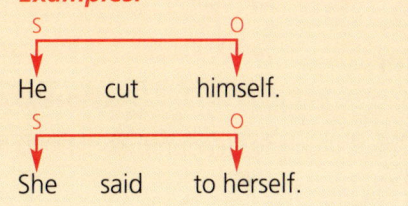

  He cut himself. (S→O)

  She said to herself. (S→O)

Table 1: *Reflexive pronouns*

Subject pronoun	Verb	Reflexive pronoun	
I		_____	
You		_____	
He		_____	
She	saw	_____	in the mirror.
We		_____	
You (plural)		_____	
They		_____	

E Read the sentences. Circle the correct word or phrase in each case.

1	Probably it was / **It was probably**	her best	novel.
2	Perhaps I'll / I'll perhaps	read it	later.
3	Sarah	said, / said us,	'I like it here.'
4	'I don't care,'	Martin	told Mary. / told to Mary.
5	Who	are you	speaking? / speaking to?
6	Lucy	told / said	Mark her phone number.
7	I taught	me / myself	English by reading.
8	Tom and Lucy asked	themself, / themselves,	'Is this really what we want?'

Grade your progress (1 = poor to 5 = very good)

At the end of Unit 3, I can:

- [ ] follow signposts in listening for giving examples
- [ ] carry out a survey into film preferences
- [ ] understand short summaries of stories
- [ ] write notes about specific information in summaries
- [ ] use the grammar of the unit accurately

Transfer

Choose one of your favourite stories and write a summary.

Reflect

Think about how language is used differently in literature. Think about your own language and how this might happen in English.

Unit 4
Sports and Leisure

Key vocabulary

activity (n)
amateur (n/adj)
birdwatching (n)
collect (v)
collection (n)
collecting (v)
collector (n)
creative (adj)
do-it-yourself (DIY) (n)
enjoy (v)
equipment (n)
fishing (n)
free time (n)
gardening (n)
hobby (n)
hobbyist (n)

interests (n)
leisure time (n)
model-making (n)
photography (n)
pleasure (n)
popular (adj)
professional (n/adj)
stamp collecting (n)
star-gazing (n)

Unit 4 Sports and Leisure

Lesson 1: Listening

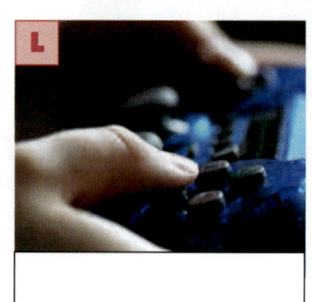

A Look at the pictures.

1 What do the pictures have in common?

2 Write the activity name under each picture.

3 Answer these questions with a partner.

   a. Which of the free-time activities are hobbies?

   b. Which are creative?

   c. Which are popular with everybody?

   d. Which are more popular with a particular age group?

   e. Which are more popular with men and which are more popular with women?

   f. Which are popular in your country?

   g. Which do you personally enjoy?

B 1:40 Listen and match each speaker with one of the pictures.

Speaker 1 ___   Speaker 2 ___   Speaker 3 ___   Speaker 4 ___

Speaker 5 ___   Speaker 6 ___   Speaker 7 ___   Speaker 8 ___

OBJECTIVES	• understand the structure of a talk	• listen to take notes
	• listen for a change of subject	

C 🔊 **1:41 Listen to the introduction to a talk about hobbies.**

1 Answer the questions.
   a. What is leisure time?
   b. Who had leisure time a hundred years ago?
   c. What simple pleasures does the lecturer mention?
   d. How does the lecturer define *hobby*?

2 What will the lecturer talk about now?

D 🔊 **1:42 Listen to the rest of the lecture.**

1 Complete the notes about model-making and photography. Write one or two words in each space.

2 Make your own notes about the other hobbies.

E 🔊 **1:43 Listen again.**

1 Put your hand up when the speaker changes subject.

2 Read the Skills Check.

F Think of some more creative hobbies. What do you make in each case?

> In photography, you make photographs.

> With gardening, you make a place beautiful.

Model-making
Making the _____ is the creative process. Most people like _____ the model, not _____ at it or _____ with it.

Photography
Photographers create a photograph, but also a _____ of _____ photographs. They put them in an album or keep them on a _____.

Do-it-yourself

Gardening

Collecting

Skills Check

Recognizing change of subject

- Sometimes speakers tell us about a change of subject.
  Example:
  Now, I'm going to talk about …

- Sometimes speakers do not tell us, but there are some clues.
  Examples:
  There are many different kinds of hobbies. For example, **model-making** is very popular.
  Many hobbies are creative. You make something. In **photography**, …
  So that's photography. What about **collecting** things?

- The speaker often says the new subject word(s) more slowly and more loudly.
- There is sometimes a pause after the subject word(s).

Lesson 2: Speaking

A Look at the pictures on page 50 again and talk in pairs. What do people enjoy about each activity?

B Look at sentences a–d below and answer the questions.

  a. When I play piano, it makes people happy.
  b. I play computer games for hours. It makes my mum really angry.
  c. The new colour made the room look nicer.
  d. Skateboarding for a few hours makes me feel good.

  1 What do all the sentences have in common?
  2 How are sentences a and b different from sentences c and d?
  3 Read Skills Check 1 and check.

> **Skills Check 1**
>
> **Uses of *make***
>
> - A common structure is *make* + object + adjective.
>   *Examples:*
>
> | Subject | *make* | Object | Adjective |
> |---|---|---|---|
> | It | **makes** | people | happy. |
> | Love stories | **make** | me | sad. |
>
> - Another common structure is *make* + object + verb. The second verb is the infinitive without *to*.
>   *Examples:*
>
> | Subject | *make* | Object | Adjective |
> |---|---|---|---|
> | Fishing | **makes** | me | relax. |
> | Comedy films | **make** | people | laugh. |

C Look at the picture.

  1 Answer the questions with a partner.
    a. What is the hobby?
    b. What do you know about this hobby?
    c. Do you know any special vocabulary for the hobby?

  2 Look at the word map for the hobby below. Write the words in the box in the correct place. Use a dictionary if you need to.

  | rod   cast   lake   bait |

equipment
- ☐ _____
- ☐ reel
- ☐ hook
- ☐ net
- ☐ _____

Fishing

verbs
- ☐ _____
- ☐ reel in
- ☐ catch
- ☐ release

places
- ☐ sea
- ☐ river
- ☐ _____

| OBJECTIVES | • talk about a personal hobby | • find and use specialist vocabulary |

D 🔊 **1:44 Listen to the man talking about his hobby.**

1 Tick (✓) the words in the word map when you hear them.

2 Answer these questions in pairs.
 a. What is angling?
 b. Why didn't the student bring a rod to show the class?
 c. What two types of fish does he mention?
 d. What different types of bait does he mention?
 e. What does he do with the fish he catches?
 f. What can you see in the pictures below? What is each for?

3 🔊 **1:45** Listen again as you read the tapescript.

E Prepare to give a talk about your favourite hobby or interest. Plan a talk of two minutes.

F Work in groups of four.

1 Take it in turns to give your talk.
2 Ask and answer questions at the end of each talk.

Skills Check 2

Specialist vocabulary

- When you give a talk or have a tutorial, you will probably need specialist vocabulary – words and phrases particular to your area of interest.
 1 Find them in a dictionary and check the pronunciation.
 2 Explain what they mean, if necessary.
 Examples:
 Angling is …   It's like a …   You use it to …
- Bring small objects to show during your talk.

Skills Check 3

Giving a talk

- Always plan a talk. Word maps (see page 52) are a good way to plan some kinds of talk.
- Find pictures of objects (or the objects themselves to show).
- Think of possible questions from other students. Can you answer all of them?

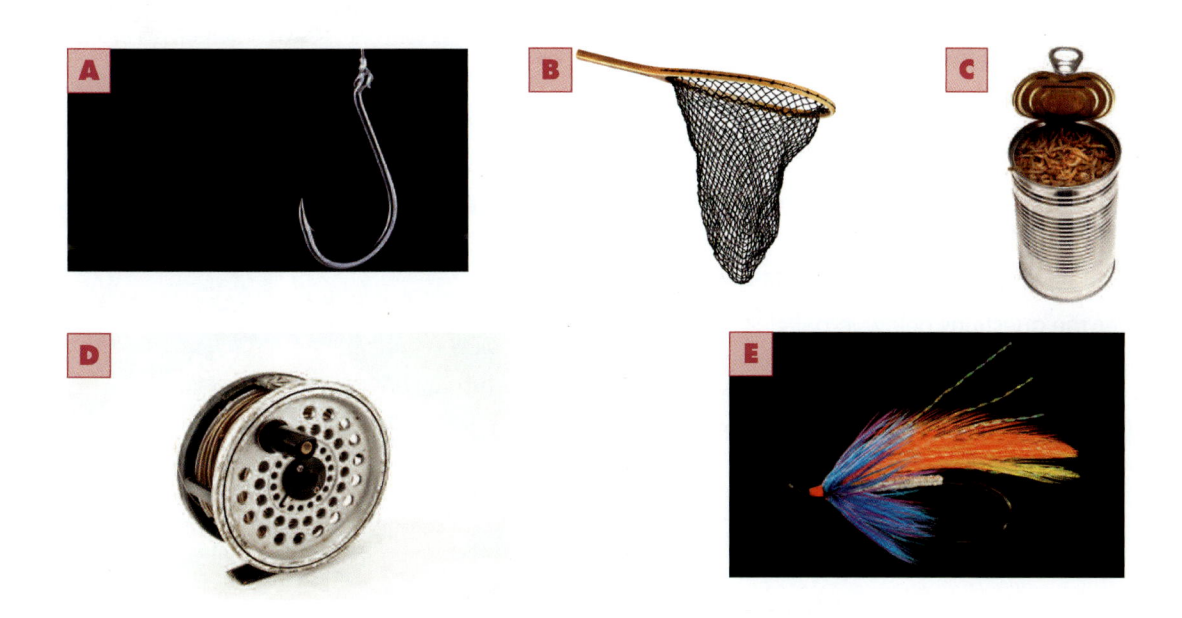

A B C

D E

English Skills for University 2b, Course Book, Unit 4

Lesson 3: Vocabulary and Pronunciation

A Study the sentences i–v in the blue box.

1 Answer the questions in pairs.
  a. How are the sentences the same?
  b. How are they different?
  c. What is the meaning of *make* in each case?

> i) I like making models.
> ii) Can I make a suggestion?
> iii) He made a hole in the wood.
> iv) It makes me happy.
> v) This music makes me want to dance.

2 Write the words in the green box into the spaces on the word map.

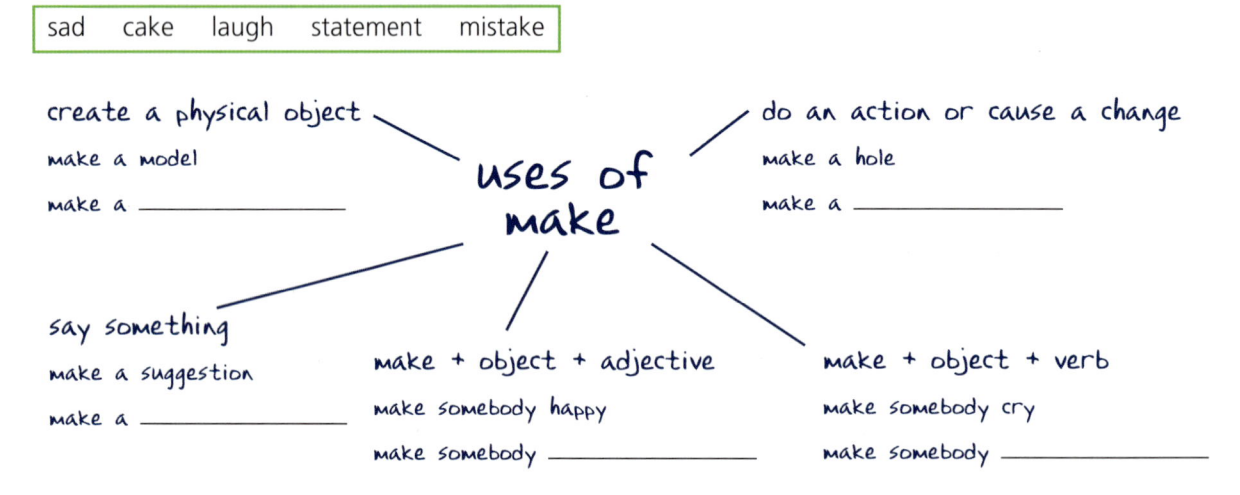

> sad   cake   laugh   statement   mistake

uses of make

- create a physical object
  - make a model
  - make a _____

- do an action or cause a change
  - make a hole
  - make a _____

- say something
  - make a suggestion
  - make a _____

- make + object + adjective
  - make somebody happy
  - make somebody _____

- make + object + verb
  - make somebody cry
  - make somebody _____

3 Work in pairs. Add one more phrase to each list.

4 Circle the correct phrases below. Correct the verbs in the wrong phrases.

make a decision / make changes / make a photo / make progress / make your homework / make money

B Study the sentences in the yellow box and answer the questions in pairs.

1 How are the sentences the same?
2 How are they different?
3 What is the meaning of *find* in each case?

> a. I found it on my desk.
> b. Many graduates can't find jobs.
> c. I found the talk very interesting.

C Study the phrases in box A.

1 Use each underlined word to complete the phrases in box B.
2 Answer the questions below in pairs.
  a. What part of speech is each underlined word in box A?
  b. Is the same word in box B the same part of speech?
  c. What are the different meanings of the pairs of words?

A	B
read a <u>book</u>	kill a _____
<u>fly</u> to New York	I _____ early
<u>play</u> a game	_____ about the weather
turn <u>left</u> here	_____ a table at a restaurant
give a <u>talk</u>	see a _____ at the theatre

54 English Skills for University 2b, Course Book, Unit 4

OBJECTIVES	• learn how words can have more than one meaning
	• learn adjectives with an ~ing or ~ed ending • pronounce words with a missing syllable

D Read Skills Check 1.

1 What are the two words in the spaces in the Word column?

2 Study the words in the box.
   a. Think of one meaning for each word.
   b. What part of speech is the word with that meaning?
   c. Think of another meaning or find one in your dictionary.
   d. What part of speech is the word with the second meaning?

| orange | lie | land | right | last | water |

E Study sentences a and b below.
   a. History is a very <u>interesting</u> subject.
   b. I'm very <u>interested</u> in history.

1 What is the difference between the underlined adjectives?

2 Read Skills Check 2 and check.

3 Circle the correct word in each sentence.
   a. Jenny was *surprised / surprising* to see her old friend at the door.
   b. They said there was a bomb. It was a very *frightened / frightening* experience.
   c. That was an *excited / exciting* football match.
   d. Most students were *satisfied / satisfying* with their exam results.
   e. I went to see the Red Hot Chili Peppers last week. They were *amazed / amazing*.

F Say the words in the box below with a partner.

| favourite | gardening | comfortable |
| vegetable | chocolate | different |

1 🔊 1:46 Listen and count the syllables.

2 What do the words have in common?

3 🔊 1:47 Listen again and tick (✓) the stress pattern for each word. Then practise saying them.

4 How many syllables do each of the ~ed adjectives below have? Practise saying them.

| bored | frightened | surprised | amazed |

5 🔊 1:48 Listen and check. Then practise saying these adjectives.

Skills Check 1

Words with more than one meaning

- Many words in English have two (or more) common meanings. The two words are often different parts of speech.
  Examples:

	Meaning	
Word	**1**	**2**
_____	opposite of right	went away from a place
_____	method of transport	practise a sport

- Some common verbs (*make*, *find*, *take*, etc.) have several different meanings.
- If a sentence does not make sense to you, think: *Do any of the words have a different meaning in this context?*
- Think about ways to organize your vocabulary notebook when you record words with different meanings.

Skills Check 2

Adjectives ending in ~ing and ~ed

- There are many adjectives in English with two endings: *~ing* or *~ed*.
  Adjective + ~ing describes the thing or person.
  Adjective + ~ed describes the feeling.
  Examples:
  a **boring** lesson / an **interesting** man
  I wasn't **interested** in it. / We were very **bored**.

	Oo	Ooo
1 favourite		✓
2 gardening		
3 comfortable		
4 vegetable		
5 chocolate		
6 different		

English Skills for University 2b, Course Book, Unit 4

Lesson 4: Reading

A Prepare to read the text on the opposite page.

Read the heading and subheading under it. Then look at the pictures.

B Cover the opposite page and work in pairs.

1 Can you remember each word for the letters in the main heading below?

'WDYTOTTAGAH?'

2 What do you think the text will be about? Tick (✓) one option below.

why people like watching television	☐
popular hobbies	☐
different types of television programme	☐

3 Read the introduction and check.

4 The two words in the box are opposites. Discuss what they mean.

| professional   amateur |

C Close the book and talk in groups of four.

1 How many hours of television do you watch in a week?

2 Do you only watch programmes you know and like? Or do you just watch what is on?

3 Do you ever watch television instead of doing a hobby or playing sport?

D Work in groups of four.

1 Choose one hobby each from the text.

2 Copy the table below in your notebook. Find key information and make notes.

Hobby	
History	
First magazine	
Hobbyists worldwide	
Why do they do it?	

3 Read the Skills Check.

4 Read your section again. Find more examples of *because*, *so*, *but* and *though*.

E Find a classmate who read about the same hobby. Compare notes.

F Return to your group of four and exchange information.

Skills Check

Reasons and concessions

• You will read more quickly if you recognize reasons and concessions. Remember how *because* and *so* give reasons. Notice how *but* and *though* make concessions.

Examples:
DIY is now very common, **but** some people only do it **because** they have no option.
'It's too expensive,' Carol told me. '**So** I do it myself. I don't like it, **though**. I make lots of mistakes.'

56 English Skills for University 2b, Course Book, Unit 4

OBJECTIVES
- predict content from a heading
- read to make notes and exchange information
- skim to check predictions
- recognize reasons and concessions

'WDYTOTTAGAH?'

(Why don't you turn off the television and get a hobby?)

Television is the most popular recreational activity in almost every country in the world. Hundreds of millions of people come home from a day at work or school and turn on the TV. But TV is not the only option. Some people have a hobby! They come home and enjoy making, collecting or looking after things. This month, Amanda Wells looks at some popular hobbies and talks to some hobbyists.

At one time, doing it yourself was normal. People painted rooms, built furniture and repaired their cars. Then people started to earn more money. They started to pay professionals to do jobs around the house. After the Second World War, things changed again. Most people did not have much money, and they did things themselves. In 1955, the first do-it-yourself magazine appeared in Britain, and in the early 60s, the first DIY programme appeared on British TV. DIY is now very common, but many people only do it because they have no option. 'I can't afford to pay someone. It's too expensive,' Carol told me. 'So I do it myself. I don't like it, though. I make lots of mistakes.' However, Carol's husband, Jimmy, enjoys DIY. 'I find it very satisfying,' he said. 'It makes me feel good.'

Gardening started soon after agriculture. Ancient civilizations in Egypt, Greece and Rome, for example, looked after gardens as well as fields of crops. Gardening and agriculture are very similar. You put something in the ground and it grows. However, there is a big difference. People grow crops because it is a necessity, but they grow and look after flowers for pleasure. Rich people in Britain had gardens a long time ago, but in the 1800s, ordinary people also started to have a small piece of ground next to their house. Gardening became a national hobby. Several magazines appeared in the 1820s. 'I love gardening because it's relaxing,' says Gill, a keen amateur gardener. 'When I'm in my garden, I don't think about work or problems.' Nowadays, gardening is one of the most popular hobbies in the world.

The first stamp appeared in Britain in 1840. It was called the Penny Black, because it was black and it cost one penny. Only twelve years later, the first magazine for stamp collectors appeared. At first, most collectors were children but, soon, adults also started collecting. Stamps spread around the world. Stamp-collecting spread, too. Nowadays, there are over 200 million stamp collectors worldwide. 'I collect stamps because they are beautiful,' says Tom. 'I also learn a lot about the world. I don't buy rare stamps, though. I'm not rich enough.' These days, a Penny Black sells for about £2,000.

A Frenchman called Niepce probably took the first photograph in June 1827. It was a picture from his window and the process took around eight hours. The word *photography* appeared in around 1839. The Greek word *photo* means 'light' and *graph* means 'writing'. At first, photography was too expensive for most people, but it still became a common hobby. A popular magazine, *Amateur Photographer*, first appeared in 1884. Nowadays, almost everyone has a camera and it is much easier to take good pictures. 'I always carry my digital camera,' Andre told me. 'I take hundreds of pictures. Photographs help me remember places and people. I find it fascinating.'

Lesson 5: Writing and Grammar

A Look at sentences a and b below. What is the difference between the grammatical forms?

a. Photography makes me happy.

b. These old photographs make me think of my grandfather.

B Answer the questions in pairs.

1 What makes you happy / sad / angry / nervous / excited?

2 What makes you laugh / cry / feel good?

C Read the e-mail. Write the words and phrases in the box in the correct space.

| I guess   well   also   though   too |

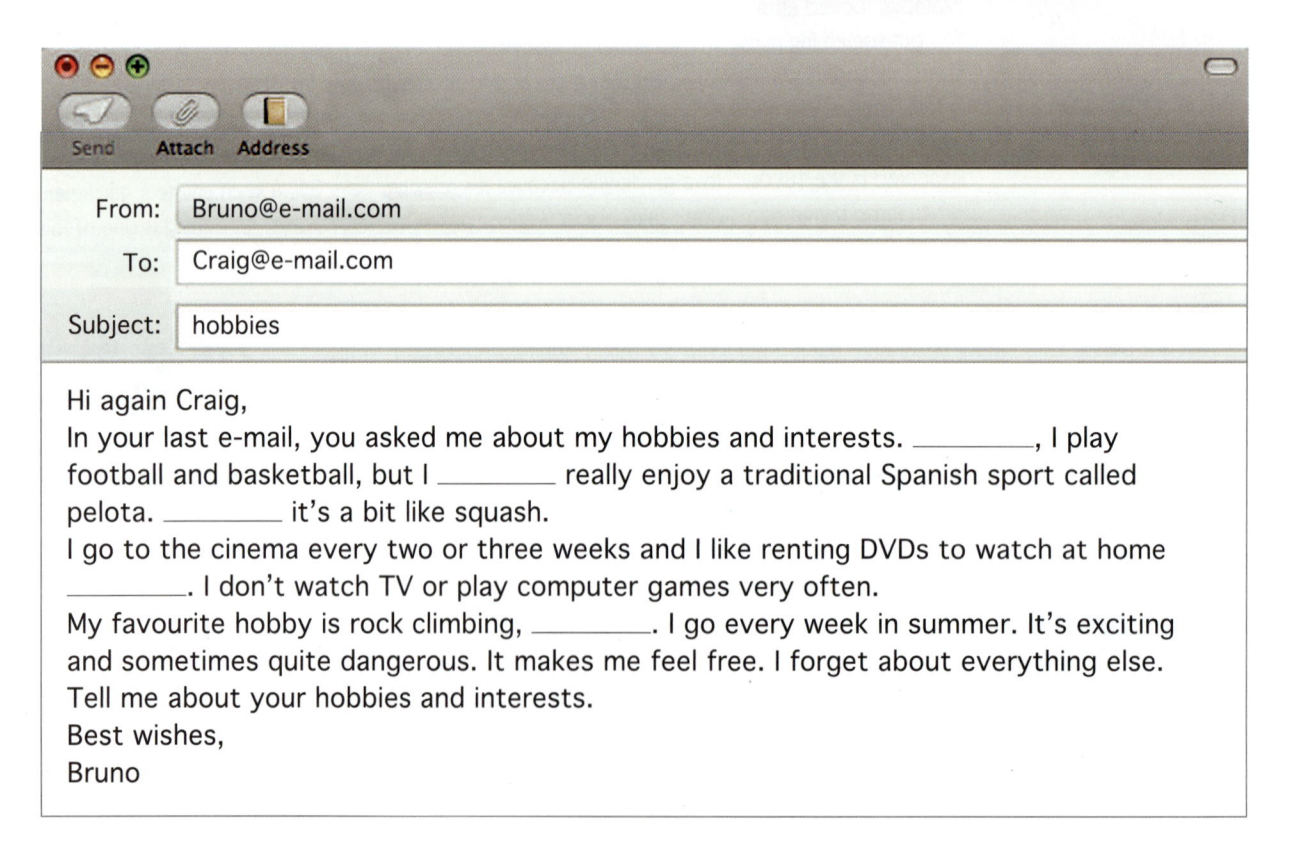

From: Bruno@e-mail.com
To: Craig@e-mail.com
Subject: hobbies

Hi again Craig,
In your last e-mail, you asked me about my hobbies and interests. _____, I play football and basketball, but I _____ really enjoy a traditional Spanish sport called pelota. _____ it's a bit like squash.
I go to the cinema every two or three weeks and I like renting DVDs to watch at home _____. I don't watch TV or play computer games very often.
My favourite hobby is rock climbing, _____. I go every week in summer. It's exciting and sometimes quite dangerous. It makes me feel free. I forget about everything else.
Tell me about your hobbies and interests.
Best wishes,
Bruno

OBJECTIVES	• learn how to use *too* and *also*
	• write an e-mail about hobbies and interests

D Study the sentences from Bruno's e-mail.

1 What do they have in common?

2 What are the differences?

> I play football and basketball, but I also really enjoy a traditional Spanish sport called pelota.

> I go to the cinema every two or three weeks and I like renting DVDs to watch at home, too.

3 Read the Skills Check and check.

4 Rewrite the sentences below using *also*.

a. Justin plays the guitar, the piano and the saxophone. He's a very good singer, too.

_____

_____.

b. We visited Japan and South Korea. We spent a night in Singapore, too.

_____

_____.

5 Write an e-mail to Bruno about your hobbies and interests.
Tell him:
- what general interests you have.
- about one specific hobby.
- why you enjoy the hobby and how it makes you feel.

Skills Check

Using *too* and *also*

- We can add information with *too* and *also*. Notice the position of each word.

  Examples:
  I am interested in reading, **too**.
  I am **also** interested in reading.

  I like tennis, **too**.
  I **also** like tennis.

  I am making a model at the moment, **too**.
  I am **also** making a model at the moment.

Lesson 6: Writing and Grammar

A Look at the pictures.

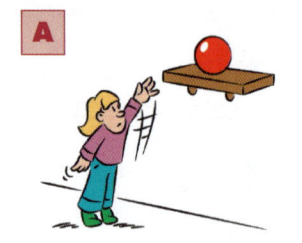

A   B   C   D

1 What is the problem in each situation?
2 Match the sentences with the pictures.

It's too hot.	
It's too loud.	
It's too big.	
It's too high.	

Table 1: very and too + adjective

S	V	Adv	Adjective
It	is	very	big.
			small.
		too	hot.
			cold.

3 Why do we use *too* and not *very* in the sentences in 2?
4 Read the Skills Check and check. Then look at Table 1.
5 Complete each sentence below with *too* and an adjective.
   a. I'm 50 now. I'm _____ for discos.
   b. Sally's only 16. She wants to learn to drive, but she's _____.
   c. $500 for a jacket! That's _____ for me.
   d. I can't do my Maths homework. It's _____.

Table 2: not + adjective + enough

S	V	Adv	Adjective	Adv
It	is	not	big	enough.
			strong	
			long	
			hard	

B Study sentence a.

   a. Sally wants to learn to drive, but she's too young.
   b. Sally wants to learn to drive, but she isn't _____.

1 Write the same idea in another way in sentence b. Use a different adjective and a different adverb.
2 Check Table 2.
3 Write full answers to the questions below in your notebook.
   a. Why couldn't Tina reach the book on the shelf?
      She couldn't reach the book because she wasn't tall enough.
   b. Why can't cows run in horse races?
   c. Why couldn't Henry calculate the equation?
   d. Why can't you make a house from paper?

Skills Check

very or *too*?
- These adverbs have a similar meaning, but there is an important difference.

| The coffee is **very** hot. | = but I can drink it. |
| The coffee is **too** hot. | = I can't drink it. (There is a problem.) |

OBJECTIVES
- learn how to use *too* + adjective
- write about the history of a hobby
- learn how to use *not* + adjective + *enough*

C Read about birdwatching. Complete the column with notes.

	Birdwatching	Stargazing (Astronomy)
History		started with civilization Anc. India (1500 BCE) studied stars/planets Aristotle (Gr. C 4th BCE) = planets round Earth (planets round Sun) Gr. 'astron' = law 'nomos' = stars
1st magazine		'Amateur Astronomer' (1929)
Why do they do it?		beautiful; sometimes find new stars/planets

D Read the notes about astronomy. Write a text.

E Do some research into your own hobby. Write a text.

Birdwatching, or ornithology, started with civilization. People in Ancient India studied birds in 1500 BCE. The Greek philosopher Aristotle named 170 types of birds in the 4th century BCE.
Nowadays, we know that there are nearly 10,000 types. The study of birds is called *ornithology*. The Greek word *ornitha* means 'chicken' and the word *logos* means 'science'.
The first magazine for birdwatchers appeared in 1859. It was called *Ibis*. People watch birds because it is relaxing. They also find the birds themselves interesting.

F Read the sentences. Circle the correct word or phrase in each case.

1	The film	made me	laugh. / laughed.
2	The sad ending	made Laura	to cry. / cry.
3	I was	bored / boring	during the film.
4	I had a	relaxed / relaxing	bath.
5	Mmm, this cake	is	very good. / too good.
6	First class travel is	too expensive / too much expensive	for most people.
7	Our hotel room	wasn't	enough big. / big enough.

English Skills for University 2b, Course Book, Unit 4

Grade your progress (1 = poor to 5 = very good)

At the end of Unit 4, I can:

- [ ] follow signposts in listening for new topics
- [ ] talk about my favourite hobby
- [ ] use linking words to improve my reading speed
- [ ] write an e-mail about hobbies and interests
- [ ] understand words with more than one meaning
- [ ] use the grammar of the unit accurately

Transfer

Think about what you enjoy watching on TV and why. Explain to a classmate.

Reflect

Think about aspects of your own language that might confuse a foreign speaker. Reflect on how this might help you with English.

Unit 5
Nutrition and Health

Key vocabulary

bag (n)
bottle (n)
box (n)
calories (n)
case (n)
cause (v/n)
decrease (v/n)
dramatic (adj)
exercise (v/n)
fall (v/n)
food poisoning (n)
fresh (adj)
fridge (n)
hard cheese (n)
gradual (adj)
healthy (adj)

increase (v/n)
jar (n)
notice (v)
piece (n)
raw (adj)
red meat (n)
refrigerator (n)
restaurant (n)
rise (v/n)
sharp (adj)
significant (adj)
slice (n)
smoke (v)
smoking (n)
soap (n)
soft cheese (n)

stand out (v)
take exercise (v)
tip (n)
toothbrush (n)
unhealthy (adj)
wrap (v)
wrapping (n)

Unit 5 Nutrition and Health

Lesson 1: Listening

A Work in pairs. Add words to the categories below.

meat	fish	fruit	vegetables	dairy	other basics
chicken	tuna	apple	potato	milk	rice

B 🔊 1:49 Listen. Write each food the speaker describes in your notebook.

C Look at Table 1.

1 Do you know all of the food items? Can you pronounce each one correctly?
2 What is the difference between *soft cheese* and *hard cheese*?
3 What is the difference between *raw* and *fresh*?
4 What do you do with food if you *wrap* it?

Table 1: *How long can you keep food for?*

Food	Days (max)
bread ■	
butter ■	
hard cheese ■ ■	
soft cheese ■ ■	
coffee ■	
eggs ■	
cooked fish ■ ■	
jam ■	
cooked meat ■ ■	
raw (fresh) meat ■ ■	
raw (fresh) fish ■ ■	
milk ■	
potatoes ■	
cooked rice ■ ■	
salt ■	no limit
tea ■	
vegetables ■	

■ wrapped   ■ in a refrigerator   ■ in a cool, dry place

OBJECTIVES
- improve prediction skills
- learn to use *too much*
- listen for statistics

D Look at the food and drink items below.

salad ___   fresh fruit ___   burgers ___
coffee ___   fruit juice ___   cola ___
milk ___   raw vegetables ___   fresh fish ___

> **Skills Check**
>
> *too much*
> - These sentences have a similar meaning, but there is an important difference.
>   He drinks **a lot of** coffee. = a large amount
>   He drinks **too much** coffee. = there is a problem
> - We use **too much** with uncountable nouns and **too many** with countable nouns.
>   *Examples:*
>   He eats **too much** red meat.
>   She eats **too many** sweets.

1 Mark each item healthy (H) or unhealthy (U).
2 Compare with a partner. Explain your answers.

> Burgers have too many calories.

> Too much coffee makes you nervous.

3 What is the difference between *a lot of* and *too much* or *too many*?
4 When do we say *too much* and when do we say *too many*?
5 Read the Skills Check and check.

E You are going to hear a short talk about food safety.

1 What can you see in the pictures? Why will the lecturer mention them?
2 We can keep fresh food and cooked food longer than ancient civilizations. Why?
3 🔘 **1:50** Listen and check. When the lecturer pauses, say the next word.

F Look at Table 1 again.

1 Which food items can you keep for a long time? Write *no limit* under *Days*.
2 Which food items can you only keep for one day? Write *1* under *Days*.
3 🔘 **1:51** Listen to the next part of the talk and check.
4 🔘 **1:52** Listen to the final part and complete the table.

English Skills for University 2b, Course Book, Unit 5

Lesson 2: Speaking

A Look at the cartoon. What do you think it is about?

B Answer the questions below in pairs.

1 What are some causes of food poisoning?
2 Where do people get food poisoning most frequently? (For example, at home/in a restaurant.)
3 Can you name any types of food poisoning?
4 Is food poisoning more or less common now?

C Look at the figures below. What does each one show?

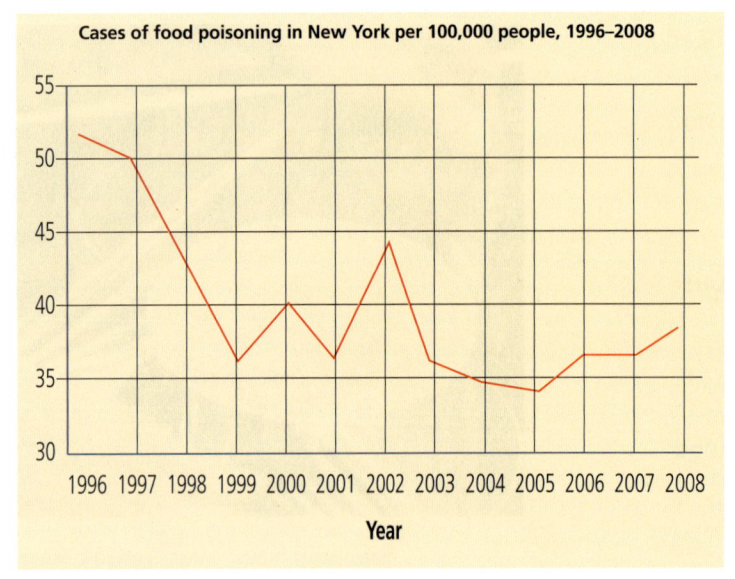

Figure 1
Source: *http://www.foxbusiness.com/on-air/stossel/blog/2009/06/11/last-night*

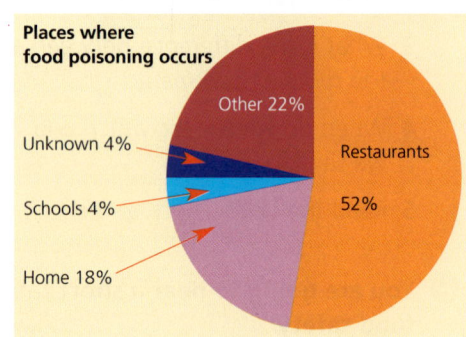

Figure 2
Source: *http://www.foodpoisoningprevention.com/ Greatest_Risk_For_Food_Poisoning.htm*

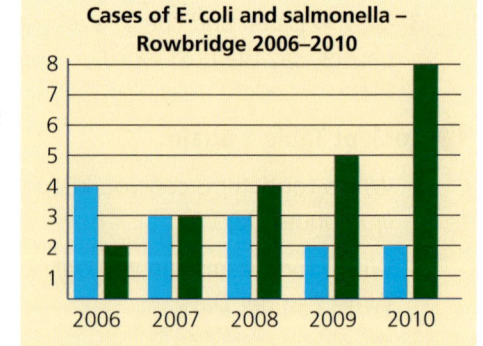

Figure 3

D 1:53 **Listen to some students.**

1 Match each extract with a figure.

Extract A ___

Extract B ___

Extract C ___

2 In pairs, try to remember some of the data the speakers described.
3 Try to remember some of their reactions to the data.

66 English Skills for University 2b, Course Book, Unit 5

| OBJECTIVES | • talk about graphs and charts | • talk about trends |

E Read the extracts below.

1 Can you remember the words in each space?
2 🔊 **1:54** Listen again and check. Write in the missing words.
3 Read the three Skills Checks.

Extract A
S1: So, what information _____ out when you look at this figure?
S2: Well, over _____ of all cases of food poisoning are in restaurants.
S1: Yes, I noticed that, too. I was quite surprised. _____ people get food poisoning at home. I guess people at home are more hygienic than people working in restaurants.

Extract B
S2: So, what about this figure? Did you _____ anything in particular?
S1: Well, cases of food poisoning _____ over the complete period. However, they _____ again at the end of the period.
S2: Yes, that's true. Why was there a dramatic _____ in 2001? Why was there a sharp _____ the next year?
S1: I have no idea. Perhaps, there was a specific problem, you know, like E. coli a few years ago.

Extract C
S1: It's _____. The number of cases of E. coli decreased over the period, while the number of cases of salmonella increased.
S2: Yes, the increase was _____ from 2006 to 2009. Then there was a _____ rise in 2010.

F Work in pairs.
- Practise Extract 1.
- Swap roles and practise again.
- What else can you say about Figure 2?
- Talk about Figure 2.
- Repeat the process with the other two extracts and figures.

G Work in groups of four.
- Go online to find a graph or chart related to nutrition and health (coffee drinking / meat eating / smoking / heart disease, etc.).
- Make a copy of the graph or chart.
- Plan your talk.
- Give a short talk.

Skills Check 1

Referring to graphs and charts

- We can describe graphs in several ways.
Examples:

Verbs	increase	decrease
	rise (rose)	fall (fell)
Nouns	an increase	a decrease
	a rise	a fall
Adjectives	slight	gradual sharp/dramatic

- We also use typical words and phrases to talk and ask about data.
Examples:
It's clear that …   What do you notice?
It's obvious that …   What stands out?

Skills Check 2

More, less and fewer

- We use *more* with countable and uncountable nouns.
Examples:
more food / **more** people
- We use **fewer** with countable nouns. We use **less** with uncountable nouns.
Examples:
less food / **less** money
fewer people / **fewer** calories

Skills Check 3

Reacting to information

- We often react to information.
Examples:
I was surprised.
The figure was surprising.

English Skills for University 2b, Course Book, Unit 5

Lesson 3: Vocabulary and Pronunciation

A **Mark the nouns below countable (C) or uncountable (U).**

cheese ___ egg ___ butter ___ carrot ___ rice ___ milk ___ bottle ___

B **Look at the pictures.**

1 What is the difference between A and B in each pair?

2 Can you think of any more pairs like these?

C **Look at the picture and read the dialogue below.**

1 Guess the words in each space. Write one or two words.

2 1:55 Listen and check.

3 Which words go with:
   a. only countable nouns?
   b. only uncountable nouns?
   c. both countable and uncountable nouns?

4 Read Skills Check 1 opposite.

M: So, what do we need?
F: Well, we're making bolognaise and pasta. We certainly need _____ meat.
M: OK, how _____?
F: It's for four people, so quite _____. Perhaps about two kilos.
M: OK, let's take this pack. It's 2.2 kilos. Do we need to buy pasta?
F: I don't think so. There's quite _____ at home. I bought _____ a few days ago.
M: What about vegetables?
F: Yes, we need tomatoes, onions and mushrooms.
M: Fresh tomatoes or in a tin?
F: Tinned tomatoes are best for bolognaise.
M: So, how _____ tins?
F: Let's get three.
M: OK, where are the fresh vegetables?
F: Over here.
M: Right, how many onions do we need?
F: _____, three or four, I guess.
M: OK, and mushrooms?
F: We need quite _____ of mushrooms. This pack looks about right. Oh, we need olive oil, too.
M: I think we've got _____ at home.
F: No, there's only _____ in the bottle. We need _____ more.
M: OK, where can we find that, then?
F: I think it's next to …

68 English Skills for University 2b, Course Book, Unit 5

OBJECTIVES
• revise and extend language related to countable and uncountable nouns
• learn about words with weak forms
• write and practise a dialogue

D Match the phrases on the left with the words on the right.

1	a bottle of	jam / marmalade / honey / peanut butter
2	a box of	bread / ham / lemon / cheese
3	a jar of	water / lemonade / wine / olive oil
4	a bag of	chocolates / biscuits / toys / tools
5	a piece of	sweets / flour / potatoes / coffee beans
6	a slice of	cake / cheese / wood / cloth

E Look at the extract below from the dialogue in Exercise C.

1 How do we say each of the underlined words?
2 What do the words have in common?
3 1:56 Listen and check.
4 Read Skills Check 2.
5 Practise the dialogue in pairs.

M: So, what <u>do</u> we need?
F: Well, we're making bolognaise <u>and</u> pasta. We certainly need <u>some</u> meat.
M: OK, how much?
F: It's <u>for</u> four people, so quite <u>a</u> lot. Perhaps about two kilos.
M: OK, let's take this pack. It's 2.2 kilos. <u>Do</u> we need <u>to</u> buy pasta?
F: I don't think so. There's quite <u>a</u> lot <u>at</u> home.

F Work in pairs. Invent a dialogue.

• Decide what you want to cook.
• Make a list of ingredients. Check any words you don't know in a dictionary.
• Write a dialogue like the one in Exercise C.
• Practise your dialogue. Make sure you pronounce weak forms correctly.
• Read your dialogue to the class.

Skills Check 1

Countable and uncountable nouns

• Nouns are either countable or uncountable. Many food nouns are uncountable.
Examples:

Countable	Uncountable
There **are** some potatoes.	There **is** some pasta.
There **are** a lot of apples.	There **is** a lot of coffee
How much milk?	**How many** eggs?
a few tomatoes	**a little** oil

• Some nouns have a countable and uncountable meaning.
Examples:
a lamb (animal)   some lamb (meat)

• We can make an uncountable noun countable.
Example
a **bottle** of water / a **glass** of juice / **piece** of cake / a **slice** of bread / a **case** of food poisoning

Skills Check 2

Weak forms of common grammatical words

• Short grammatical words often have a weak form in conversation.
Examples:
do /də/
and /ən(d)/
of /əv/
for /fə/
some /səm/

English Skills for University 2b, Course Book, Unit 5 **69**

Lesson 4: Reading

A Cover the text on the opposite page.

1. Read the heading and subheading of the text below.
2. What is a *tip*?
3. What do you think the top five tips will be? Compare your ideas with other students.

HOW CAN I STAY HEALTHY?

We asked 100 doctors for their tips on staying healthy.
Here are the top five tips and some research results with each tip.

B Read the headings of each section below.

1. What is the missing key word in each one?

   DON'T _____

   DON'T EAT TOO MANY _____

   DON'T LIE IN THE _____

   TAKE _____ **EVERY DAY**

   GO TO BED _____ **TWICE A WEEK**

2. Look at the text and check your answers.
3. What will the advice be in each section?

C Work in groups of five.

1. Choose one piece of advice each. Find the key information and make notes under the headings opposite.
2. Guess words from context or look them up in a dictionary.

D Read the Skills Check.

E Read your text again. Do you believe it?

F Work in topic groups. Find other students with the same advice. Compare your notes.

G Return to your group of five. Ask about the other advice. Explain new words.

Topic	
General advice	
Research results	
Who said?	
When?	
My opinion	

Skills Check

Doing research: *Who said? When?*

- The Internet is a good place to find information. But ask yourself:

True?	What is the source?
New?	What is the date? Newer information is often better.
Research?	Is there research, or just statements?

70 English Skills for University 2b, Course Book, Unit 5

OBJECTIVES
- predict information about known subject before reading
- predict from headings and subheadings
- read to take notes and exchange information

HOW CAN I STAY HEALTHY?

We asked 100 doctors for their tips on staying healthy.
Here are the top five tips and some research results with each tip.

1. DON'T SMOKE

Smoking harms you, your friends and your children. It also makes your clothes smell terrible! If you smoke a lot, it will probably kill you. Research has shown that …

> … smoking harms nearly every part of the body (National Cancer Institute, USA, April, 2004). It kills 5 million people worldwide every year (WHO, 2003). If you live with a smoker, you will also smoke. There is a 24% rise in the chance of getting lung cancer (British Medical Journal, 1997).

2. DON'T EAT TOO MANY SWEETS

We all need sugar, but if you eat lots of sweets, you will probably get bad teeth. You will probably get fat, too. Research has shown that …

> … if you are very fat, you will probably get a serious illness. Thirty different illnesses are linked to obesity (National Health and Nutrition Examination Survey, USA, 1988–1994). Another study shows that dark chocolate may prevent cancer and heart disease (Dutch National Institute of Public Health, 1997). But don't eat too much!

3. DON'T LIE IN THE SUN

We need sunlight to make Vitamin D, but too much sun is very dangerous. If you sunbathe regularly, you may get skin cancer. In Australia, 1,250 people die every year from skin cancer. Research has shown that …

> … skin cancer in Norway rose 350% for men and 440% for women between 1957 and 1984 (Norwegian Cancer Institute). People started to use sun cream in the 1960s and 70s. Professor Moan of the Institute says, 'People think that sun cream makes them safe. But it is not true.'

4. TAKE EXERCISE EVERY DAY

You don't have to spend hours in the gym. If you walk for half an hour a day, you will help your body to work properly. You will also feel better. Research has shown that …

> … half an hour's exercise makes your heart stronger (American Heart Association). Research with mice has shown that exercise can also make memory better. Perhaps the results are true for humans, too. 'Just one month of exercise changed the brainpower of the mice,' said researcher Fred Gage (Journal of Neuroscience, 20th September, 2005).

5. GO TO BED EARLY TWICE A WEEK

Sleep is very important. If you get an average of eight hours a night, you will help your body to function properly. Research has shown that …

> … if you are tired, you are less efficient and you will perform some actions less well. In the USA, over 1,500 deaths happen on the roads each year because the driver falls asleep at the wheel (National Highway Traffic Safety Administration, USA, 1999).

Lesson 5: Writing and Grammar

A

You mustn't smoke.

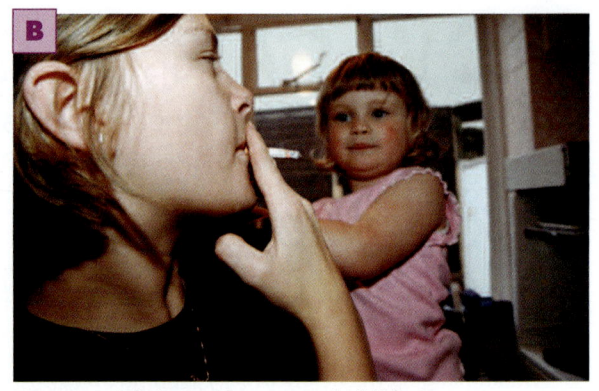

B

You shouldn't smoke around children.

A Look at the pictures.

1 What is the difference between *must* and *should*?
2 Look at Table 1.

B Alfie is very unhealthy. He is at the doctor's. Complete the doctor's advice. Use *should* or *shouldn't* and some of the verbs in the box.

drink	increase	smoke	help	stop	take
	watch	eat	play		

1 You _____ smoking.
2 You _____ so many burgers.
3 You _____ more exercise.
4 You _____ TV all day.
5 You _____ more water.

Table 1: Should + *infinitive*

Subject pronoun	Modal	Verb
I		
You		
He	should (not)	smoke.
She		
We		
They		

C Give advice to a person visiting your hometown.

> You should visit the cathedral. It's beautiful.

D Match the sentence beginnings with the sentence endings.

1	If you live in a hot country,	you shouldn't drive.
2	If you live in a cooler country,	you can't learn to drive.
3	If you're under 17,	you can drink less water.
4	If you're very tired,	you increase the chance of heart disease.
5	If you eat a lot of red meat,	you need more water.

E Study the completed sentences in Exercise D. Answer the questions.

1 What do the sentences have in common?
2 Do the sentences express fact or possibility?
3 Can the beginnings and endings be the other way round?
4 Look at Tables 2 and 3.

Table 2: *Conditionals expressing fact (1)*

If	S	V	Other	S	V (Modal)	Other
If	you	live	in a hot country,	you	need	more water.

Table 3: *Conditionals expressing fact (2)*

If	S	V	Other	S	V (Modal)	Other
	You	need	less water	if	you	live	in a hot country.

72 English Skills for University 2b, Course Book, Unit 5

OBJECTIVES	• learn *should* / *shouldn't* + infinitive	• learn conditionals expressing fact (zero)
	• learn conditionals expressing possibility (first)	• write giving hygiene advice

F Match the sentence beginnings with the sentence endings.

1	If you smoke near children,	you probably won't survive.
2	If you join a gym,	it will go bad.
3	If you're in a plane crash,	they may copy you.
4	If you keep food too long,	you may develop skin cancer.
5	If you eat too much unhealthy food,	you will probably get fat.
6	If you lie in the sun for too long,	you will feel healthier.

G Study the completed sentences in Exercise F. Answer the questions.

1 What do the sentences have in common?
2 Do the sentences express fact or possibility?
3 Can the beginnings and endings be the other way round?
4 When do we use *will* and when do we use *may*?
5 Why do we add *probably* to some sentences?
6 Look at Table 4.

Table 4: *Conditionals expressing possibility*

If	S	V	Other	S	Modal	Adverb	V	Other
If	you	lie	in the sun,	you	will / may	probably	develop	skin cancer.

H Complete each sentence with a possibility.

1 If you drive when you're tired, you …
2 If you eat a lot of fruit and salad, you …
3 If Tommy eats only burgers and chips, he …
4 If Tracy doesn't do any exercise, she …

I Read about washing your hands. Complete the column with notes.

J Read the notes about brushing your teeth. Write a text.

Topic:		brush your teeth after eating and drinking
General advice		many health problems → germs; toothpaste kills germs; so brush after eating/drinking; if food in teeth = go bad
Research results		use a soft toothbrush; brush = 3 mins; most people = 1 min
Who said?		The American Dental Association
When?		2005

wash your hands with soap

Many health problems start with germs. However, soap kills germs so you should wash your hands after using the toilet. If you wash your hands with soap, you will kill billions of germs.

Research has shown that regular washing could save a million lives a year. *(London School of Hygiene and Tropical Medicine, 2003)*

Lesson 6: Writing and Grammar

A **Study Table 1.**

1 Put ticks (✓) in the correct columns. Sometimes you need to tick both columns.

2 Tick (✓) the correct sentences. Correct the wrong ones.

Table 1: *Countable and uncountable nouns and related language*

Words	Countable *potato/es*	Uncountable *cheese*
is		✓
are	✓	
much		
many		
some		
How much?		
How many?		
a lot		
a few		
a little		
more		
less		
fewer		
too much		
too many		

a. How many homeworks does your teacher give you?
b. I don't have much money for my holiday.
c. People in China eat more rice than people in Europe.
d. People in China eat less potatoes than people in Europe.
e. You only need to put a few salt in the soup.
f. Too many people use mobile phones when they're driving.

B **Look again at the graph from Lesson 2 on the next page.**

1 Complete the first part of the report opposite with one word in each space.

2 Write the second part of the report.

74   English Skills for University 2b, Course Book, Unit 5

OBJECTIVES	• revise countable and uncountable nouns and related language • write a report of information in a graph

The graph shows how _____ people per 100,000 people in New York got food poisoning each year between 1996 and 2008. Cases of food poisoning _____ over the complete period, but _____ again from 2005 to 2008. Between 1996 and 1999, there was a _____ fall in the number of food poisoning cases in the city. Between 1999 and 2000, there was a _____ rise in the number of cases. Then, between 2000 and 2001, the number of cases fell again.

Cases of food poisoning in New York per 100,000 people, 1996–2008

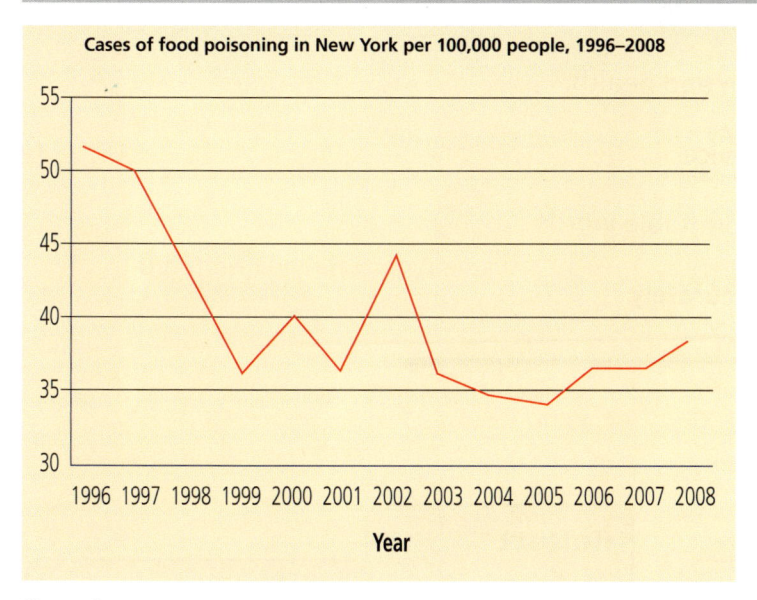

Figure 1
Source: http://www.foxbusiness.com/on-air/stossel/blog/2009/06/11/last-night

C Read the sentences. Circle the correct word or phrase in each case.

1	Tina eats	too much / too many	chocolate.
2	Less / Fewer	people eat red meat	these days.
3	I like	many / a lot of	sugar in my tea.
4	Would you like	a piece of	cake? / cakes?
5	You shouldn't	eat / to eat	too many burgers.
6	You can't vote	if	you are not 18. / you will not be 18.
7	If you smoke, / If you will smoke,	you may	develop lung cancer.
8	If you develop lung cancer,	probably you will / you will probably	die.

English Skills for University 2b, Course Book, Unit 5

Grade your progress (1 = poor to 5 = very good)

At the end of Unit 5, I can:

- [ ] predict what a speaker is going to say
- [ ] plan and give a talk on nutrition and health
- [ ] write a short piece of health advice
- [ ] understand countable and uncountable words
- [ ] use the grammar of the unit accurately

Transfer

Search the Internet for any health-based information. Explain the content to a classmate.

Reflect

Reflect on how you can use *if* clauses to think about cause and effect. Come up with as many examples as you can.

Review

Review

Lesson 1: Listening

A 🎵 **2:1** Listen to some sentences about the topics you learnt about in Units 1–5. Mark them true (T) or false (F).

1 ___ 2 ___ 3 ___ 4 ___ 5 ___ 6 ___ 7 ___ 8 ___ 9 ___ 10 ___

B Look at the pictures and answer the questions in pairs.

1 What is the difference between the two types of cinema?

2 What type of films do you think each cinema shows?

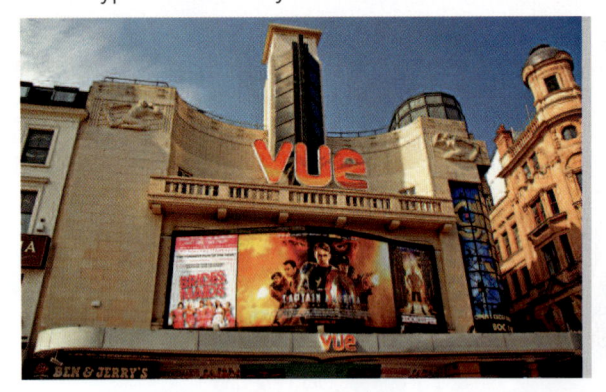

C 🎵 **2:2** Listen to the first part of a radio interview. Answer the questions in pairs.

1 What type of film does the cinema show?

2 What type of film does the cinema not show?

3 What else did you learn about the cinema?

D 🎵 **2:3** Listen to the rest of the interview and complete Table 1.

Table 1

Type of film	Typical audience
	students
love story	
	women
crime	
	men
foreign language	

E Did you understand the words and phrases below from the context?

- Hollywood blockbuster
- screen
- subtitles

F Do you have small independent cinemas in your country? Do you go to them?

G 🎧 **2:4 Listen to the introduction to a lecture about diet.**

1 Which two diets is the lecturer going to compare?
2 What do you think he will say about each food item in the pictures?

H 🎧 **2:5 Listen to the first part of the lecture. Mark the sentences true (T) or false (F).**

1 Red meat has more fat than chicken. ___
2 Chicken is very good for you. ___
3 Fat in the blood is dangerous for the heart. ___
4 Japanese people eat more fish than we do in the West. ___
5 People in the West have more heart attacks than Japanese people. ___
6 Japanese people eat a lot of butter. ___

I 🎧 **2:6 Listen to the second part of the lecture. Complete the notes. Use one or two words in each space.**

Changes to diet
mostly economic – people spend _____ on more food, but people don't eat _____

In Japan
more meat / less fish / more hamburgers and so more _____

In the West
less fish – reduction in fishing so _____ prices
more convenience food (hamburgers, pizzas & food we put in the _____)
food not healthy – too much fat and _____

J Is the typical diet changing in your country?

Lesson 2: Speaking

A Talk in pairs. What is happening in each picture?

B Choose one picture.

1 When did you last experience an event like this?
2 Tell your partner about it.

C Talk in pairs. Compare the methods of transport in the blue box. Use each of the words in the yellow box.

| car   motorbike   bicycle   bus   train   plane   boat | more   fewer   less |

> There are fewer accidents on trains than in cars.

D Work in pairs.

Student A: Look at the questions in Box B and prepare answers. Ask your partner the questions in your box.
Student B: Look at the questions in Box A and prepare answers. Ask your partner the questions in your box.

Box A	Box B
1 What's your favourite film?	1 What's your favourite book?
2 What type of film is it?	2 What type of story is it?
3 Which actors/actresses are in it and who directed it?	3 Who wrote it?
4 Where and when is the story set?	4 Where and when is the story set?
5 How does the story start?	5 What happens?
6 Who is the main character and what does he/she do?	6 How does the story end?

E Work in groups of four.

1 Choose one free-time activity from the pictures below.
2 Plan a short talk. You should talk for a minute.
3 Look up key vocabulary. Make sure you can pronounce the words correctly.
4 Take it in turns to talk about your activity.

F Look at Figure 1.

1 Check any words you don't know. Make sure you understand them.
2 Talk about the information in pairs.

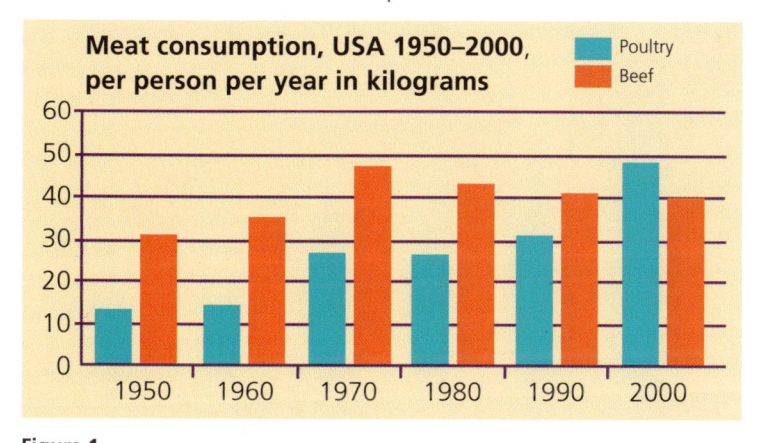

Figure 1
Source: http://www.admc.hct.ac.ae/hd1/english/graphs/bar_meat_ans.htm

G Study the conversations.

1 Complete each conversation with a word in each space.
2 2:7 Listen and check your answers.
3 Role-play the conversations in pairs.
4 Add some more lines to each conversation.

Conversation 1
A: Do most people _____ married in church in your country?
B: Yes. People are not always religious, but they still like a church ceremony.
A: Do most people have a traditional white _____?
B: Oh yes. The bride usually wears a white _____.
A: What happens after the church ceremony?
B: Well, …

Conversation 2
A: Did you fly?
B: Yes, I did.
A: How was the _____?
B: It wasn't very good, actually …

Conversation 3
A: Who's your _____ film character of all time?
B: Err, that's a difficult question. I think it's _____ Darth Vader, you know, in *Star Wars*.
A: Oh, really? He's a _____ character.
B: Yes, I find heroes a bit boring. What about you?
A: I …

Conversation 4
A: What do you like doing in your _____ time?
B: Well, I like reading and listening to music, but I _____ my real hobby's surfing.
A: Really? How _____ do you go surfing?
B: _____ week in the summer. We drive to the beach. Last year, I went surfing in Hawaii _____. What about you? What's …

Conversation 5
A: So, what do we need for this omelette?
B: Well, we need eggs.
A: OK, how _____?
B: Well, it's for three people, so let's say four.
A: Do we need milk?
B: Yes, but just a _____. We mix that with the eggs.
A: OK, then …

English Skills for University 2b, Course Book, Review 81

Lesson 3: Vocabulary and Pronunciation

A **Correct the spelling mistakes in the underlined words.**

1 Are Tim and Sally going to cristen the baby? _____
2 It's Jack and Lynn's Golden Wedding Aniversery next year. _____
3 Did you have a good jurney? _____
4 There was a bad aksident on this corner last week. _____
5 Catwoman is my favourite Batman caricter. _____
6 Sherlock Holmes solved many misteries. _____
7 I thought the film was very fritening. _____
8 People get a lot of plezure from their hobbies. _____
9 Fried food has a lot of kalories. _____
10 People get food poisening if they don't keep food fresh. _____

B **Write the opposite of each word or phrase.**

1 high _____   5 fast _____
2 rising _____   6 happy _____
3 safe _____   7 interesting _____
4 comfortable _____   8 soft _____

C **Match each verb with a noun or noun phrase.**

1	make	a firework display
2	take	a crime / a mystery
3	watch	a question
4	give	a job
5	ride	a mistake
6	have / cause	presents
7	answer	a role
8	play	a fish
9	solve	a photograph
10	paint	a bicycle
11	catch	a room
12	find	an accident

D **Find one word that has the two meanings below.**

Example: a) you read it b) reserve a seat or table   _book_

1 a) a colour   b) a fruit   _____
2 a) not the front   b) part of your body   _____
3 a) look at   b) it tells you the time   _____
4 a) use money   b) fill time   _____
5 a) go by plane   b) insect   _____

E Look at the words in the left column below.

1 Find a word in the right column with the same (underlined) vowel sound.

2 2:8 Listen and check.

1	g<u>o</u>		j<u>our</u>ney
2	c<u>u</u>stom		l<u>au</u>gh
3	br<u>i</u>de		n<u>ow</u>
4	d<u>ea</u>th		gr<u>ou</u>p
5	s<u>a</u>fe		w<u>a</u>ter
6	f<u>a</u>st		p<u>i</u>lot
7	cart<u>oo</u>n		l<u>o</u>ve
8	res<u>ea</u>rch		f<u>a</u>vourite
9	f<u>ou</u>nd	/	r<u>o</u>le
10	sp<u>or</u>t		m<u>e</u>n

F Look at the words in the left column below.

1 Tick (✓) the column with the correct stress pattern.

2 2:9 Listen and check.

3 Say the words with the correct pronunciation.

		Ooo	oOo	Oooo	oOoo	ooOo
1	ceremony			✓		
2	anniversary					
3	celebrate					
4	population					
5	comfortable					
6	competition					
7	adventure					
8	historical					
9	literature					
10	photography					
11	dramatic					
12	ingredients					

Lesson 4: Reading

A Answer the questions below in pairs.

1 What makes you happy?
2 When are you happiest?
3 Who are you happiest with?

B Prepare to read the text on the opposite page.

1 The text has three sections. Look at the three headings below. What do you think the whole text is about?

Something to Aim for
Someone to Talk to
A Little of Everything

2 Read the introduction and check your ideas.
3 Read the three section headings again. What do you think each section is about?

C Read the whole text quickly and write each section heading into the correct place.

D Look at the underlined words and phrases in the definitions below.

1 Find each word or phrase in the text and try to understand it from the context.
2 Circle the correct option in each definition.

a. If you worry, you feel that something *good / bad* will happen.
b. If you waste time or money, you use it *well / badly*.
c. Chores are *little jobs / enjoyable activities*.
d. If you set a target, you *have a clear idea of what you want / think about the future too much*.
e. If you achieve something, you *do it / can't do it*.
f. Material possessions are *objects you have / things you think about*.
g. Luxuries are things you *really need / don't really need*.

E Read each section and choose the best summary.

A Little of Everything	Something to Aim for	Someone to Talk to
Do everything quickly.	Be organized.	Don't be lonely.
Enjoy everything you do.	Aim for the best.	Luxury is not important.
Don't waste time and money.	Wait for tomorrow.	You don't need a Ferrari.

F Talk in groups. Which person do you agree with? Why?

All Saints College *Opinions Page*

Another Week, Another Opinion

How To Be Happy

This week we ask: How can you live a happy life? We asked our readers to tell us. Perhaps we can learn a thing or two from them!

How can you be happy, and live a long time? I know the answer. It's simple. Don't worry about anything. Don't waste time choosing healthy food or worrying that something may be bad for you. However, you shouldn't have too much of anything. Also, don't waste money buying things you don't need. Don't spend money on exercise bikes or expensive clothes. Do your chores around the house, but do them as quickly as you can. Try to tidy your room, make the beds and wash the dishes in less than an hour. Next day try to do it in 50 minutes. It's all good exercise and it's fun. My grandfather gave me this advice. He's 104 and he's still healthy and happy!

Veronica

It is easy to be happy. There are so many problems in the world and we all need to work hard to find happiness. Organize your time. Leave time for all the little jobs that you don't like, but need to do. Plan days, weeks, months and even years ahead. Set yourself targets. When you achieve those targets you'll feel fantastic. Sometimes you won't succeed. Don't worry. See it as a new opportunity. Try to achieve more next time. I work very hard and one day soon, I'll achieve my ambitions. If it isn't today, it'll be tomorrow. I'm nearly 30 and I'll soon be a happy woman. I know it's going to happen.

Sandra

Many people aren't happy because they are always looking for something. We spend our lives studying and then working. We want money to buy things. We think they will make us happy. But do they really? Do material possessions make us happy? Will driving a new Ferrari make you a better person? Do you really need a TV with a bigger screen?

We should be happy with food on the table, a home to live in and a family to share it with. I live in a small house and I haven't got a car or a computer. I eat simple meals and I don't need luxuries. All I need is people to talk to. Am I happy? Well, I was yesterday before my girlfriend left me.

Mick

Lesson 5: Writing and Grammar

A Read the phrases below.

1 What is the topic?

2 Compare ideas with a partner.

- stamps, matchboxes or old bottles
- all sorts of things
- in many different ways
- is collecting
- but they usually do it because the design is attractive or interesting
- collect old tickets from sports games or rock concerts

3 Read the phrases below. Make sentences by joining them to the phrases above.

a. people spend their free time
b. a popular hobby
c. people collect
d. Some people collect
e. Others
f. collectors may collect strange things

B Put all the sentences in order to make a paragraph. Add punctuation.

_____
_____
_____
_____
_____

C Work in pairs.

1 Talk about your hobbies.

2 Make notes about your favourite hobby.

3 Write a paragraph about your hobby.

D Tick (✓) the correct sentences. Correct the wrong ones.

1	Not many babies are born at home these days.	
2	The population rises in most African countries.	
3	What did happen at the party last night?	
4	When people get married, friends and relatives usually buy a present.	
5	One way to measure road safety is to look at the number of accidents on a particular road.	
6	How was your hotel like?	
7	Jim was driving too fast and he was losing control of the car.	
8	Wait a moment. I'm speaking to my sister on the phone.	
9	Suzy taught himself to play the piano. She didn't have any lessons.	
10	*Psycho* probably is Alfred Hitchcock's best-known film.	
11	The end of the film made me to cry.	
12	Can we find a cheaper restaurant? This one is too much expensive.	
13	I'm going to go home and have a relaxing bath.	
14	He won't be a professional footballer. He isn't good enough.	
15	I found the part of the lecture about the Romans very interested.	
16	A lot of people eat too much red meat these days.	
17	We've got chickens and rice for dinner.	
18	If you are from Belgium, you can probably speak French.	
19	People really shouldn't to use bad language when children are listening.	
20	If you will not take exercise, you will get unhealthy.	

Lesson 6: Portfolio

A Prepare for the task.

Look at the pictures on the opposite page.

1 What is each activity?

2 What are the attractions and benefits of each activity?

3 Which of the activities are expensive and which are quite cheap?

4 Do you need to buy any special equipment for each activity?

B 2:10 **Listen. Which activity is the speaker talking about?**

C 2:11 **Listen again and complete the notes.**

D Answer the questions.

1 When is the speaker sometimes frightened?

2 Who shouldn't try caving?

E Would you like to try caving? Why/why not?

F Work in groups of four. You will try to persuade the other students in your group to try an activity.

- Each student chooses one of the other activities on the opposite page.
- Go online to find information and make notes.
- Make a note of any key vocabulary you need.
- Plan to talk for about two minutes.
- Use pictures to make your talk more interesting.

G Take it in turns to give your talk.

- Try to persuade the other members of your group that your activity is the best.
- Decide together which student in the group gave the most persuasive talk.

Caving
(in U.S. also called _____ / in UK also called _____)

What it involves
exploring underground _____ and caves
(Perhaps discovering a _____ cave)

Reasons to do it
it's very _____ – not too _____ if careful
it's very sociable – work with other people as a _____ / learn to _____ people – you make _____
it's not too _____ – club may have some equipment

English Skills for University 2b, Course Book, Review 89

Unit 1 Culture and Civilization

Listening and Speaking

1 important symbol – people know person with ring is not _____
2 custom started – Ancient _____ – rings made from plants from River _____
3 Roman times – custom of engagement ring (_____ of marriage) started
4 not always only symbol of _____ – also part of groom's fortune
5 Friend or maid looked after rings – this person now called _____
6 20th century – _____ also started to wear ring

A You are going to hear a lecture about wedding rings.

1 Look at a student's notes above. Predict information to complete the notes.

2 🔊 **1:1** Listen to the lecture. Write one or two words into each space.

3 Look at the words below. Did you hear them in the lecture? Did you understand them from the context?

| reeds | eternity | engagement | purse | maid |

4 🔊 **1:2** Listen again and check.

5 Use each word to complete the sentences.
   a. A _____ is a small bag, usually for money.
   b. A _____ works for a rich family or in a hotel.
   c. People give _____ rings when they decide to get married.
   d. _____ is time with no beginning or end.
   e. _____ are plants from a river.

B 🔊 **1:3** Listen to sentences from a lecture about birthdays.

1 Number the best word or phrase to complete each sentence. You don't need all the words.

   Example: *1 A 16th birthday is very important in many cultures because the person becomes …*

   forty.   ☐   a mother.   ☐
   the school.   ☐   a new house.   ☐
   party.   ☐   dinner.   ☐
   fifty.   ☐   smoke.   ☐
   vote.   ☐   thirty.   ☐
   an adult.   [1]   the door.   ☐

2 🔊 **1:4** Listen and check.

90 English Skills for University 2b, Workbook, Unit 1

C Listen.

1. **1:5** Respond to each sentence you hear.

   Example:

   You hear: *Most babies are born at home.*

   You say: *Actually, most babies are born in hospital. / Most babies are born in hospital, actually.*

2. **1:6** Listen again and write a response below.

   a. Actually, _____.

   b. _____, actually.

   c. Actually, _____.

   d. _____, actually.

D Read the short conversation below.

1. Write one of the phrases from the box in each space.

   | I think so   that's right   I'm not really sure   I see |

   A: Are you from Germany?

   B: Yes, _____. How did you know?

   A: I heard your accent.

   B: Oh, _____. Where are you from?

   A: Italy. My name's Marco.

   B: Hi, I'm Hans.

   A: So, is the lecture in this room?

   B: _____, but _____. There aren't many other students here.

   A: No, I'm going to ask somebody.

   B: OK, I'll wait here.

2. **1:7** Listen and check.

3. Practise the conversation in pairs.

Reading and Writing

A Complete the table with words from the Course Book unit.

Noun	Adjective	Verb
		be born
		christen
		die
		marry / get married
celebration		
weight		
tradition		

B Correct the spelling mistakes.

1 aniversery _____

2 serimony _____

3 funrel _____

4 gests _____

5 preyer _____

6 perade _____

C Read about a famous person in Western culture.

1 What is her full name?

A Famous Life

She was born in 1961. Her family name was Spencer. She was not very good at school and she left when she was only 16. In 1979, she started work in a pre-school. In 1981, she got married. Her husband was called Charles Windsor.

She had two sons. William was born in 1982, and Harry was born in 1984. However, her marriage was not a good one and she and Charles separated in 1992. She started to do a lot of work for poor people. On 31st August, 1997, she died in a car accident in Paris. She was 36 years old.

2 Make notes in Table 1 opposite.

Table 1: *A woman's life*

b.	
name	
left school	
first job	
m.	
children	
d.	

D **Look at Table 2.**

1 Have you heard of him?

Table 2: *A man's life*

b.	1491
name	Henry Tudor
first job	King of England (1509) = Henry VIII
m.	Catherine of Aragon (1509) Anne Boleyn (1533) Jane Seymour (1536) Anne of Cleves (1540) Catherine Howard (1540) Catherine Parr (1543)
children	Mary (1516) Elizabeth (1533) Edward (1537)
d.	1547 (age 56)

2 Use the information to write about him. Use the text in Exercise C1 as an example.

3 Make notes about a famous person from your country in Table 3.

Table 3

b.	
name	
life	
m.	
children	
d.	

4 Use your notes to write about the person.

Unit 2 They Made Our World

Listening and Speaking

A You are going to hear about some transport accidents.

1 Read the pieces of information below. Find four types of information.

- Dag Hammarskjöld
- Pierre Curie
- boat
- motorcycle
- car
- 31/08/1997
- 19/04/1906
- plane
- Paris, France
- T E Lawrence
- pedestrian
- Ndola, Zambia
- 17/09/1961
- 13/05/1935
- Dorset, England
- Livorno, Italy
- Diana, Princess of Wales
- Percy Bysshe Shelley
- 08/07/1822

2 Write the types of information as headings for the first four columns of Table 1 below.

Table 1: *Deaths of famous people in transport accidents*

				What happened?

3 Do you know anything about any of the people?
   a. How did they die?
   b. When did they die?
   c. Where did they die?

94 English Skills for University 2b, Workbook, Unit 2

B Listen.

  1 **1:8** Write information in the first four columns of the table. You can use the same information more than once.

  2 Think about what you can write in the final column.

C **1:9** Listen again. Write notes about each accident in the final column of the table.

D **1:10** Listen to some sentences from the recording. Can you understand the underlined words from the context?

  1 Photographers were <u>chasing</u> the car on motorcycles.

  2 Pierre was crossing the road in Paris when the wheel of a <u>carriage</u> hit him.

  3 There were two children on bicycles on the road. He <u>swerved</u> to miss them and crashed.

  4 It is possible that Hammarskjöld survived the crash, but he was dead when <u>rescuers</u> found him.

  5 There was a terrible storm and the boat sank. Shelley <u>drowned</u>.

E Choose one of the accidents. Tell a partner what happened in your own words.

F **1:11** Listen to two conversations. Answer the questions.

  1 How did each speaker travel?

  2 What was the journey like?

G **1:12** Listen again and complete the conversations below.

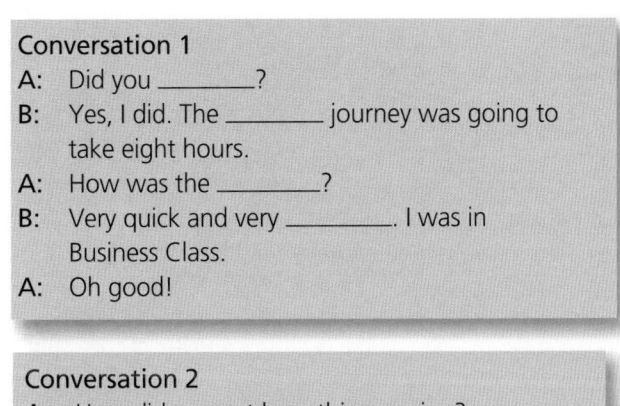

Conversation 1
A: Did you _____?
B: Yes, I did. The _____ journey was going to take eight hours.
A: How was the _____?
B: Very quick and very _____. I was in Business Class.
A: Oh good!

Conversation 2
A: How did you get here this morning?
B: On the _____.
A: How was the journey?
B: _____, actually. There were no _____.
A: Oh dear.

H Practise the conversation in pairs.

Reading and Writing

A Scan the two texts on the opposite page. What are the texts about?

B Read the text about Amelia Earhart.

1 Complete her column in Table 1.

2 Mark information on the map. Show routes and dates.

Table 1: *Two deaths*

	Amelia Earhart	Amy Johnson
born		
died		
nationality		
bought a plane		
became a pilot		
what happened to her?		

C Check that you understand the words below.

> transport (v)   foggy   off-course

96   English Skills for University 2b, Workbook, Unit 2

Amelia Earhart

Amelia Earhart was born on 24th July, 1897, in Kansas in the United States. When she was 18, she had a ten-minute flight in a plane and loved it. She did a number of different jobs to pay for flying lessons. She bought her own plane in 1920 and got her pilot's licence in 1923.

In 1932, she flew across the Atlantic on her own. She was the first woman to do this. The journey took 15 hours and 18 minutes. At the age of 40, she decided to fly around the world. She took one other person, Fred Noonan. His job was to plan the route.

The first part of the flight was fine. They took off on 17th March, 1937, from California and flew to Florida. Then they crossed the Caribbean to South America. From there, they flew across the South Atlantic to Africa, over the Sahara Desert, around the tip of Arabia and on to India. From India, they flew to Australia.

Next they had to fly 4,000 kilometres to a small island in the middle of the Pacific Ocean. They took off on 2nd July, 1937. They never arrived. Where did they go? Nobody knows. The government of the United States spent $4 million looking for the plane, but never found it.

Amy Johnson

Amy Johnson (born) ____ 1st July, 1903, ____ Hull in the United Kingdom.

She (be) interested ____ flying as a girl ..... (get) her pilot's licence ____ 1929. She (can) not get a job ____ a pilot ..... she (study) to be an engineer. In 1930, her father (buy) her a plane ....., in the same year, she (become) the first woman to fly from England ____ Australia. The journey (take) 19 days. In 1931, she (fly) from England to Japan, ... in 1932 from England to South Africa.

She (marry) another famous pilot, Jim Mollison, in 1932. They (fly) together to the United States, ... the plane (crash) in Connecticut. They both (survive).

The Second World War (start) in 1939. In 1940, Amy (get) a job transporting planes around the United Kingdom. ____ January 5th, 1941, the weather (be) very cold ..... foggy. Amy (take) a plane ____ Blackpool in the northwest of England to Oxford in the centre ____ the country. She (crash) into the sea near London. Why (be) she so far off course? Nobody knows. She (survive) the crash, ... (drown) ..... rescuers (arrive). She (be) 37 years old.

D Read the text about Amy Johnson. Write the complete text in your notebook.
- Put the verbs in brackets into the correct past form.
- Complete spaces ____ with prepositions.
- Complete spaces ..... with *and*, *but* or *so*.

E Complete Amy's column in Table 1 and mark her routes with dates on the map.

F Close your books and talk in pairs. Find five things that Amelia and Amy had in common.

Unit 3 Media and Literature

Listening and Speaking

A **Look at the film posters.**

🎧 **1:13** Listen to some people talking about the films below. Match the number of the speaker with the film posters.

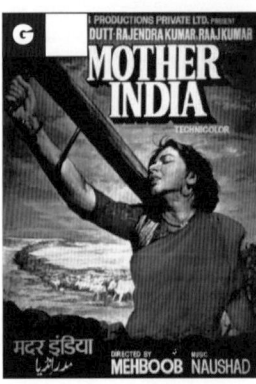

A.
B.
C.
D.
E.
F.
G.
H.

98 English Skills for University 2b, Workbook, Unit 3

B Talk about each film in pairs.

   1 Guess the answers to these questions.

     a. What type of film is it?

     b. What time in history is it set?

     c. What happens in the film?

     d. How does it end?

   2 Which film would you most like to see? Why?

C Look at the questions below. Think of a suitable reply.

   1 How often do you go to the cinema?

   2 What sort of films do you like?

   3 What about love stories?

   4 When did you last go to the cinema?

   5 What did you see?

   6 Was it good?

   7 What was it about?

   8 How did it end?

D Look at the answers below.

   1 Match the answers to the questions in Exercise C.

   2 1:14 Listen and check.

     a. Yeah, I quite like them.

     b. Oh, they all lived happily ever after, of course.

     c. It was a comedy, actually.

     d. Once or twice a month.

     e. Yeah, it was really very funny.

     f. A group of friends. They go on holiday to South America and lots of silly things happen.

     g. Adventure and science fiction.

     h. A couple of weeks ago.

   3 Practise the questions and answers in pairs.

E Have a real conversation about films. Use the questions from Exercise C.

Reading and Writing

A Scan the text opposite.

1 What is it about?

2 What do you know about this story already?

B Read the first paragraph and look at the picture. Discuss these questions.

1 What does the picture show?

2 Who is the man in white?

3 Where is the creature?

4 Where will the electricity come from?

5 What do you think happens next in the story?

C Work in groups of six.

1 Read one of the paragraphs, A–F.

2 Complete the table below for any new words in your paragraph.

3 Try to work out the meanings from context.

Word	Part of speech	Meaning

D Cover the text.

1 Explain what happens in your paragraph.

2 Explain the new words in your table.

3 Work out the correct order of the paragraphs.

4 Uncover the text. Check your order.

E Talk in your group. What do we learn from Frankenstein's story?

F Look at the picture and the first paragraph again.

1 Write this part of the story as a narrative. Use past tenses.

Victor Frankenstein was in his laboratory. This was the moment ...

2 Compare your story with other students.

Frankenstein
by Mary Shelley (1818)

Victor Frankenstein is a young scientist. He learns how to make a living creature from body parts. He brings it to life with electricity. He wants it to be beautiful, but it is ugly and frightening. The creature wants Frankenstein to love him, but Victor hates the creature and runs out of his laboratory.

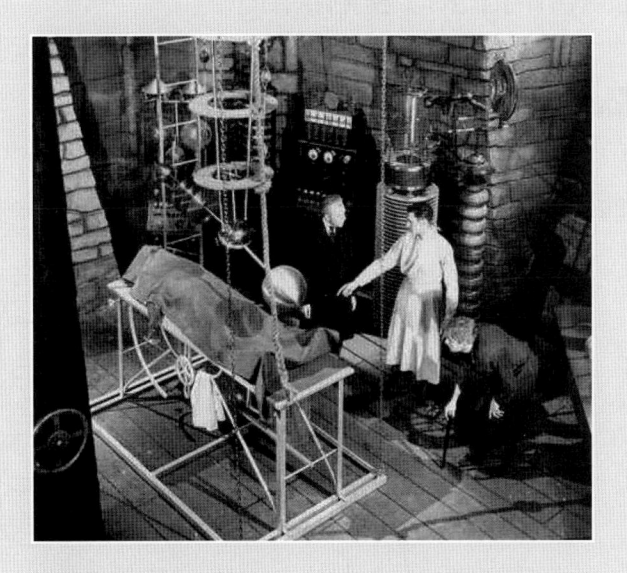

A Frankenstein agrees and starts to make another creature. Suddenly, he realizes that two creatures will be worse than one. They could have children. He destroys the second creature, but the first one is watching. 'I will be with you on your wedding night,' the creature tells Victor.

B Frankenstein decides to kill the creature on his wedding day, but the creature is too clever. He kills Elizabeth and runs away. Frankenstein goes mad and follows the creature for hundreds of kilometres, to the North Pole. Finally, Victor dies in the snow and ice.

C Frankenstein returns later, but the creature is not there. Victor is happy and goes back to his normal life. He meets a woman, Elizabeth, and they decide to get married.

D Meanwhile, the creature is lonely and wants a wife, too. By now, he can use human language. He learns by listening to people while he is hiding on a farm. He finds Frankenstein and asks for his help.

E The creature is sad after Victor's death. 'I will not kill again,' he says. 'I will go out into the cold, and die.' At the end of the story, the creature walks into the snow and disappears.

F Then a horrible thing happens. Someone, or something, kills Frankenstein's young brother, William. The police arrest a young girl for the murder. Victor knows the creature is the killer, but he does not say anything. The police think the girl is guilty and they execute her.

Unit 4 Sports and Leisure

Listening and Speaking

A 🎧 **1:15 Listen to some sentences.**

1 Number the best word or phrase to complete each sentence. You don't need all the words.

Example: *1 I watched a horror film last night. I was very …*

exciting. ☐	too. ☐
enough. ☐	cry. ☐
laugh. ☐	amazed. ☐
amazing. ☐	excited. ☐
hobby. ☐	frightening. ☐
frightened. [1]	very. ☐

2 🎧 **1:16 Listen and check.**

B 🎧 **1:17 Listen to some sentences. Tick (✓) the correct meaning of the words.**

Example: *1 The bank is on the right opposite the cinema.*

1 right	a) correct	☐	b) not left	✓
2 land	a) come down to the ground	☐	b) country	☐
3 free	a) no cost	☐	b) not busy	☐
4 talk	a) speak	☐	b) lecture	☐
5 fly	a) insect	☐	b) travel	☐
6 matches	a) games	☐	b) small sticks for making fire	☐

C You are going to hear a lecture about the Romans and their leisure time.

1 Check the words and phrases opposite in a dictionary before you listen.

| board   game   dice   counters   hunting   mask |
| amphitheatre   chariot   bathe (v) |

2 Look at a student's notes opposite. Predict information to complete the notes.

3 🎧 **1:18 Listen to the lecture. Write one or two words in each space.**

102 English Skills for University 2b, Workbook, Unit 4

Board games
What were the _____?

Hunting
Romans hunted for _____.
Introduced _____ to countries they occupied.

Theatre & amphitheatres
In plays, actors and actresses wore masks of a good or bad _____.
In amphitheatres, gladiators fought each other or with _____.

Chariot racing
Chariot racers were celebrities - like footballers. They became _____.

Roman baths
Romans spent all day in _____ baths.
They did exercises, swam and bathed.
Rich Romans conducted _____ at the bathhouses.

D **Look at the jumbled conversations.**

1 Put the sentences in each conversation into the correct order.

Conversation A
a) What kind of models?
b) Have you got any hobbies?
c) Well, I'm interested in cars.
d) Yes, I make models.

Conversation B
a) What kind of films do you watch?
b) I like going to the cinema.
c) Anything really, but I really like horror films.
d) What do you do in your free time?

Conversation C
a) Are you good at it?
b) Do you play any sports?
c) No, but I like playing.
d) Not much. I play a little tennis.

Conversation D
a) So, how do you relax?
b) What do you do in the evenings?
c) I watch TV or read a book.
d) Not much, I'm usually too tired.

2 **1:19** Listen and check.

3 Practise the conversations in pairs.

Reading and Writing

A Scan the texts opposite.

1 What are they about?

2 What do you think about this subject?

B Read the introduction. What does the text do? Tick (✓) one or more.

gives advice	☐
gives information	☐
makes you think	☐
says 'television is bad'	☐

C Work in groups.

1 Read two or three pieces of information each. Learn the information.

2 Complete Table 1 with any new words in your information. Work out the meanings from context.

3 Cover the text. Tell the group your information and words.

4 Which piece of information is different from all the rest?

Table 1: *New words*

word	n, v, adj	meaning

D Read the other pieces of information. Did you understand the information correctly?

E You are going to write a short article entitled 'Television is bad for young children'.

1 Make a list of points. Write the number of the piece(s) of information next to each point in Table 2. The first one is done for you.

2 Number your points in order (1 = most important).

Table 2

points	information	order
TV and video games may slow down development.	3	
Children see violent acts and copy them.		
Children become frightened of the real world.		
Children don't know adverts are adverts.		
Too much television makes you fat.		
Children see bad habits and copy them.		

F Write your article.

1 Copy the introduction to the article.

2 Write the rest of the article in your notebook in your own words.

Is television bad for young children?

Discussion Point

Young children in most countries watch a lot of television, but do they watch *too much*? Do young children learn from television or is it bad for them? In this week's Discussion Point, we look at evidence from the United States, including the American Academy of Pediatrics (AAP). Decide what you think.

1 Most children watch television before they start school. Seventy per cent of centres for children under five use TV to entertain the children.

2 According to the AAP, schoolchildren in the United States watch about four hours of TV a day. In a year, the average schoolchild spends 900 hours in school, but nearly 1,023 hours in front of a TV.

3 According to the AAP, children under two should not watch TV or play video games because television can slow down the development of very young children. The child does not explore or play with parents and other children.

4 Television can help very young children to learn the alphabet and can teach them about the world, including animals, nature and other children.

5 If a child watches more than four hours of TV per day, he will probably get fat.

6 The average American child sees more than 200,000 violent acts (e.g., murder) on television by the age of 18. Many of these violent acts are by 'good guys', for example, policemen, not 'bad guys'. Some children will copy the violent acts.

7 According to research, children between two and seven are frightened by monsters on television. You cannot tell them, 'It's OK. It is not real.' They do not know the difference between real and not real at that age.

8 News programmes are often full of violent pictures, e.g., crashes, murders. Parents want their children to know about the world, but these pictures can frighten young children. If a child watches programmes about crimes, including murder, he will probably become frightened of the world.

9 Television programmes often show people with bad habits, for example, smoking. Some children will copy these habits when they see them on television.

10 According to the AAP, children in the United States see 40,000 advertisements each year, including adverts for junk food and sweet drinks. Children under eight do not know the difference between an advert and a programme.

Unit 5 Nutrition and Health

Listening and Speaking

FOOD can make you ill!

Did you know …?

over _____ people in the USA get FOOD poisoning every year.

nearly _____ Americans die from FOOD poisoning every year.

Remember!
- Keep raw FOOD _____
- Don't keep FOOD _____
- Wash your hands _____
- Wash your hands _____
- Cook FOOD _____
- Eat FOOD _____

Fact:
One bacterium in FOOD can become _____ bacteria in 7 hours

A Look at the poster.

1 Read the title of the poster. What is the poster about?

2 Read *Did you know …?* Guess the missing numbers.

3 Read *Remember!* Try to complete each piece of advice.

B 1:20 Listen to the introduction. Fill in the missing numbers in *Did you know …?*

C 1:21 Listen to the next section. Think about the advice in *Remember!*

D 1:22 Listen and complete each piece of advice.

E 1:23 Listen and complete the *Fact*.

106 English Skills for University 2b, Workbook, Unit 5

F Read the sentences in the box.

Good idea. If we don't book, we might not get a table.	Thanks very much.
Fish with tomatoes and black olives.	Are you frying the fish?
~~Can I have a ham and salad sandwich, please?~~	Oh, brown, please.
~~Let's go out for dinner this evening.~~	Here you are.
Would you like some mayonnaise?	~~Would you like some more soup?~~
Just a little. I'm quite full.	White or brown bread?
~~What are you cooking? It smells delicious.~~	Yes, why not? I'll book a table for eight.
OK. Do you want to try the new Italian place?	No, I'm baking it in the oven.

1 Check any words you don't know.
2 Make four conversations.
3 **1:24** Listen and check your answers.

Conversation 1

A: Can I have a ham and salad sandwich, please?

B: _____

A: _____

B: _____

Conversation 2

A: Would you like some more soup?

B: _____

A: _____

B: _____

Conversation 3

A: What are you cooking? It smells delicious.

B: _____

A: _____

B: _____

Conversation 4

A: Let's go out for dinner this evening.

B: _____

A: _____

B: _____

G Practise the conversations in pairs. Continue each conversation with two or three more sentences.

Reading and Writing

A Prepare to read the text on the opposite page.
   1 Scan the text. What is it about?
   2 What do you know about this subject already?
   3 What vocabulary related to this topic do you know?

B Read the introduction. What are the subsections of this text, e.g., campylobacter?

C Work in groups of four.
   1 Read about one of the bacteria.
   2 Complete the column of Table 1 for that bacteria.
   3 Use a dictionary to check any key words and phrases that you don't know.

D Cover the text.
   1 Tell your group about your bacterium.
   2 Listen and make notes about the other bacteria in the appropriate columns in Table 1.

Table 1: *Common food poisoning bacteria*

Bacteria	How serious?	Foods	Solution
campylobacter			
salmonella			
listeria			
E. coli			

E Read about the other bacteria. Did you understand the information correctly?

F Cover the text. Write about one of the other bacteria in your notebook.

How can I make my food safe?
This week: *Killing the bacteria*

One cause of food poisoning is bacteria. In fact, bacteria cause about 65% of all cases of food poisoning. The main bacteria are campylobacter, salmonella, listeria and E. coli.

Campylobacter
This bacteria is very common in chickens. In fact, it is present in more than half the chickens in the United States. You can also get the bacteria from raw milk – that is, milk straight from the cow. Milk producers do not sell raw milk. They sell pasteurized milk (see inset). If you cook chicken properly, you will kill the bacteria. Over 2.5 million Americans suffer from campylobacter each year. Most people recover, but around 125 die.

Salmonella
Salmonella is common in raw or badly cooked eggs. It is also present in about a quarter of the chickens in the US. We also find it in raw meat and dairy products, like milk, butter and cheese. You will kill salmonella if you pasteurize milk before you make butter or cheese (see inset). You will also kill it if you cook food properly. Salmonella is the source of only 10% of food poisoning cases around the world, but it causes the most deaths. In the United States, 30 people die from salmonella poisoning every year.

Listeria
Listeria is in the water around us. It can occur in dairy products, including ice cream, and in fast foods, like hot dogs and burgers. It also appears in raw fish and raw meat. We can even get listeria poisoning from vegetables. If you cook meat for long enough at a high temperature, you will kill the listeria bacteria. You will also kill the listeria bacteria if you pasteurize the milk for ice cream (see inset). Only about 2,500 people in the US get listeria poisoning each year, but 15 die. Listeria is responsible for about 28% of all deaths from food poisoning.

E. coli
E. coli is sometimes present in fast foods, like hot dogs and burgers, but it can also appear in apple juice, if the juice is not pasteurized (see inset). If you cook meat for long enough at a high temperature, you will kill the E. coli bacteria. If you pasteurize juice, you will also kill the E. coli bacteria. Most forms of this bacteria are harmless, but some forms are very dangerous. If you eat just ten bacteria of these forms, you will be very ill and you may die.

Pasteurizing
Pasteurizing is a method of making milk and other liquids safe to eat. It is named after the French scientist, Louis Pasteur. He invented the method in 1862. Pasteurizing involves heating a liquid to 72 degrees Celsius for 15 seconds.

Review

Listening and Speaking

A Listen.

1. 🔊 **1:25** Number the best word or phrase to complete each sentence. You don't need all the words.

   Example: *1A 16th birthday is very important in many cultures because the person becomes …*

jump. ☐	street. ☐	raw. ☐
laugh. ☐	party. ☐	problems. ☐
fresh. ☐	clean. ☐	festival. ☐
crashes. ☐	life. ☐	arrives. ☐
lands. ☐	cry. ☐	
an adult. [1]	work. ☐	

2. 🔊 **1:26** Listen and check.

B Listen.

1. 🔊 **1:27** Respond to each sentence you hear.

   Example:

   You hear: *Most babies are born at home.*

   You say: *Actually, most babies are born in hospital. / Most babies are born in hospital, actually.*

2. 🔊 **1:28** Listen again and write a response below.

   a. Actually, _____.

   b. _____, actually.

   c. Actually, _____.

   d. _____, actually.

C Read the sentences 1–4, which come from lectures. Match each sentence with a lecture feature a–d.

1. During the ceremony, the groom – that's the man getting married – puts a ring …
2. One way to measure safety is to … another way is to …
3. Most people like historical dramas, like *The King's Speech* or *Braveheart*.
4. The second point I want to mention is …

   a. A lecturer will sometimes help us to predict the structure of a talk. ☐

   b. A lecturer usually prepares us for a change of topic. ☐

   c. A lecturer will sometimes explain a word that he or she thinks you will not understand. ☐

   d. A lecturer often uses a word or phrase, then gives an example. ☐

D Look at the everyday expressions in the box.

1 Write each expression into a space in the short conversations below.
2 🔊 **1:29** Listen and check.
3 Practise the conversations.

> I'm not really sure.
> Oh good!   That's right.
> Oh dear.   How was it?
> I think so.   OK, why not?

A: What time does the film start?
B: _____ There are usually advertisements first.
A: I'll ask at the desk.

A: Let's go and see a film tonight.
B: _____ Is there something you want to see?
A: The new Julia Roberts film looks interesting.

A: You study medicine, don't you?
B: Yes. _____ I'm in my second year.
A: I study literature.

A: I went to a job interview this morning.
B: _____
A: Not bad. I think they liked me.
B: _____

A: Does this word mean 'not expensive'?
B: Yes, _____ I'll check in my dictionary.
A: Thanks.

A: Was your journey OK?
B: Actually, it was terrible. There was a lot of traffic.
A: _____

E Work in pairs.

1 Take it in turns to choose a topic from below.
2 Your partner must talk about it for 30 seconds without pausing!

a famous person's wedding
a famous person's funeral
a present you received
flying
learning to drive
a book you really enjoyed
a character from a film
how not to be bored
a dangerous hobby
staying healthy
your favourite actor/actress

Reading and Writing

A **Put commas in the sentences below where necessary.**

1 Thousands of years ago in pre-history there were many dangers and people only lived for about 20 years.
2 In the Renaissance at the time of Michelangelo and Shakespeare most people lived until they were 37.
3 There are thousands of accidents every day involving trains pedestrians cars and planes.
4 His passenger a soldier called Richer fell out of the car and died three days later in hospital.
5 Doyle was born in Edinburgh Scotland in 1859 and died in 1930 aged 71.
6 In each story something strange happens and Holmes a private detective solves a crime.
7 At one time doing it yourself was normal. People painted rooms built furniture and repaired their cars.
8 Research has shown that if you are tired you are less efficient and you will perform some actions less well.

B **Look at the extracts below.**

Read the extract, think about the meaning of the underlined word or phrase in context and tick (✓) the correct definition that follows.

a. Close family members often follow the hearse in their cars.
   A *hearse* is …
   i) a box. ☐   ii) a ceremony. ☐   iii) a kind of car. ☐

b. People know this corner as an accident black spot. Last year, there were several bad accidents, including one that resulted in the death of a cyclist.
   A *black spot* is …
   i) a safe place. ☐   ii) a dangerous place. ☐   iii) a bad driver. ☐

c. I like to get the cinema early so I can watch all the trailers before the main film starts. They usually show four or five trailers.
   Trailers are …
   i) extracts that advertise films. ☐   ii) people working in a cinema. ☐   iii) long films. ☐

d. A lot of people, especially men, take up golf when they get to around 40. Perhaps they feel too old for more physical activities, and they think golf is more relaxing.
   Take up means …
   i) stop an activity. ☐   ii) start a hobby. ☐   iii) grow older. ☐

e. These days, people eat a lot more processed meat, like ham and bacon. It keeps for longer, but it may be connected with health problems. If you want to eat meat, you should eat fresh meat whenever possible.
   Processed means …
   i) fresh. ☐   ii) expensive. ☐   iii) not natural. ☐

C Read the summary of a very famous story called *Jane Eyre*.

1 Decide where the verbs in the box go in the story.

2 Write them in the spaces in their correct form.

| help teach see go love work leave meet try fall |

Jane Eyre is a girl from an ordinary family. When she _____ school, she _____ to find a job teaching children. She _____ as a private teacher in a big house. She _____ English and other subjects to a young French girl. She soon _____ the master of the house, Mr Rochester. He is also the girl's father. One day, Jane _____ for a walk. She _____ Mr Rochester riding his horse. Suddenly, he _____ from his horse and Jane _____ him. She begins to understand that she _____ Mr Rochester.

D Join each pair of sentences in two ways, as in the example.

Example: He / drive down / steep hill   wheel / break

He was driving down a steep hill when a wheel broke.
A wheel broke when he was driving down a steep hill.

1 plane / land   fire started / one engine

_____
_____

2 I / eat / hard sweet   break / tooth

_____
_____

E Complete the text about stamp collecting. Write one word in each space.

The first stamp appeared in Britain in 1840. It was called the Penny Black, _____ it was black and it cost one penny. Only twelve years later, the first magazine _____ stamp collectors appeared. _____ first, most collectors were children _____ soon adults also started collecting. Stamps spread around the world. Stamp-collecting spread, too. Nowadays, there are over 200 million stamp collectors worldwide. 'I collect stamps because _____ are beautiful,' says Tom. 'I also learn a lot about the world. I don't buy rare stamps, though. I'm not rich _____.' These days, a Penny Black sells for about £2,000.

COURSE BOOK Transcript

Presenter: 1:1
Unit 1: Culture and Civilization
Lesson 1: Listening
Exercise B1. Match each sentence to a life event.

Voice:
1 The average age for a woman to get married in the United States is 27.
2 In some cultures, a funeral is usually no more than 24 hours after a person dies.
3 In South Korea, only 1% of births are at home.
4 In many countries, a traditional white wedding is still the most popular option for a marriage.
5 Twenty-five per cent of babies are born early, 70% are born late and only 5% are born on the date that they are due!
6 More people visit Michael Jackson's grave than any other in the world.

Presenter: 1:2
Exercise B2. Listen again. Identify a key word or phrase for each life event.
[REPEAT OF TRACK 1:1]

Presenter: 1:3
Exercise C. Listen to a short lecture about life and culture in the UK. Make notes in the *customs* column of the table.

Lecturer: Everybody is born and everybody dies. Most people get married at some time in between. These three life events, birth, marriage and death, are important in almost all cultures. I'm going to give you some information about each of these events in the UK and tell you about some special customs that are typical.

Most babies are born in hospital, rather than at home. Mothers feel the environment is safer. Sometimes women choose to have a second or third baby at home. Most babies are born late and around a third are born early – did you know that only 5% of babies are born on the date they're due? It's usual for friends and family to send a card and buy a present when a baby's born. People often buy baby clothes or a soft toy, like a teddy bear. Most families christen their babies within a year or two of their birth. The ceremony is called a christening.

Most women in the UK get married before they're 30. Men generally get married a little later. A traditional white wedding in a church is still the most popular type of ceremony. Friends and family celebrate a day that they'll always remember. During the wedding ceremony, the groom – that's the man getting married – puts a ring on the bride's finger. He puts it on the third finger of her left hand. The best man usually keeps the ring until the moment he passes it to the groom in the church.

A funeral is typically three to six days after a person dies, but can sometimes be later. When people go to a funeral, they wear black and often bring or send flowers. The family of the dead person usually buys a gravestone to mark his or her grave. They put the person's name and the date of his or her birth and death on the stone. They often put a sentence

	about the person too. Close family and friends visit a person's grave regularly.
Presenter:	**1:4** **Exercise F2. Listen and check.**
Voice:	a. Cuba has a very high marriage rate at 17.7 per 1,000 people. b. Africa is the continent with the highest death rate at 14 per 1,000 people. c. The birth rate in North America is 14 per 1,000 people, while in South America, it is 21.5.
Presenter:	**1:5** **Exercise G1. Listen and write numbers in the boxes.**
Lecturer:	Marriage is a very popular institution all over the world, but there are significant differences in marriage rates. For example, while Cuba has one of the highest rates at 17.7 per 1,000 people, Argentina has a rate of just 3.9. Three point nine is, in fact, the world's lowest marriage rate. The Philippines is a country that also has a very high rate. It's close behind Cuba with a rate of 14.2. In many countries in Western Europe, people seem less enthusiastic about getting married. The UK has a marriage rate of 5.9, while France has one of the lowest rates at 4.4. A number of countries have a rate around 10. Bangladesh has 10.7, Egypt has 9.2 and the USA has 8.9. Syria has a slightly lower rate of 8.6. The world's most populated country, China, has a marriage rate of 7.7.
Presenter:	**1:6** **Exercise I1. Listen and write numbers in the boxes.**
Lecturer:	There are significant differences between birth rate and death rate in different continents. Africa has the highest birth rate at 39 births per 1,000 people, but also has the highest death rate – 14 per 1,000 people. Europe has the lowest birth rate at 10.5 per 1,000, but a fairly high death rate, too, at 12. So, why does Europe have a high death rate? Well, it's because Europe has an ageing population. That means a lot of people are old – nearly 20% of people in Europe are over 65 years old. There are big differences in the birth rate in the Americas. In North America, the birth rate is 14, while in South America, it's 21.5. The death rates are very similar, however. North America has a death rate of 8.5 and South America, 7.5. In Asia, the birth rate is 20.5, so slightly below the rate in South America. In Australasia, the birth rate is a little lower at 18. At 8 per 1,000, Asia and Australasia have the same death rate.
Presenter:	**1:7** **Exercise J3. Listen and check.**
Lecturer:	The world's population is growing simply because the birth rate is higher than the death rate. Overall, the world birth rate is 22 and the death rate is 9. The difference, then, is 22 minus 9, which is 13 per 1,000 people, or 1.3%. There are significant differences, however, between the growth rates in different continents. In Africa, for example, the difference between the birth rate and death rate is 23,

	whereas in Europe, it's -1.5. We can see, then, that the population of Europe isn't rising at all – it's actually falling.
Presenter:	1:8
	Lesson 2: Speaking
	Exercise B. Listen to part of a tutorial. Which event above are they talking about?
S1:	I researched a *festival*. It's called the Day of the Dead.
S2:	Is it a funeral?
S1:	No, not really. It's a day to remember dead friends and relatives.
S2:	Does it happen every year?
S1:	Yes, that's right. It's on the first and second of November.
S2:	Where does it happen?
S1:	In Mexico, certainly, but I think it happens in Nicaragua and so on.
S2:	Is it popular?
S1:	Yes, very popular.
S2:	What happens exactly?
S1:	People visit graves and say prayers. They tell stories, they sing and they dance. They go to the graveyards. They often take the favourite food and drink of the dead person. They take toys for dead children.
S2:	So, is it a celebration?
S1:	Yes, exactly. It's a day to be happy. There are parades through the streets. People wear costumes or carry figures of dead people.
S2:	When did the custom start?
S1:	I understand that it started hundreds of years ago, at the time of the Aztecs.
Presenter:	1:9
	Exercise C3. Listen to the tutorial again and check your answers. [REPEAT OF 1:8]
Presenter:	1:10
	Exercise D2. Listen and check your ideas.
Voice:	a. Is it a funeral? b. Does it happen every year? c. What happens exactly? d. Is it a celebration? e. When did the custom start? f. Is it popular?
Presenter:	1:11
	Exercise E2. Listen and check your ideas.
Voice:	a. No, not really. b. Yes, that's right. c. In Mexico, certainly. d. Yes, very popular. e. What happens exactly? f. I understand that it started hundreds of years ago.
Presenter:	1:12
	Lesson 3: Vocabulary and Pronunciation
	Exercise A3. Listen and check your answers.
Voice:	a cake a christening a costume a honeymoon a parade a present candles fireworks a speech an anniversary
Presenter:	1:13
	Exercise B2. Listen and check.
Voice:	a. take part in a parade b. cut a cake c. go to a christening d. go on honeymoon e. wear a costume f. blow out candles g. give a present

	h. watch fireworks
	i. make a speech
Presenter:	1:14
	Exercise C2. Listen and repeat the questions.
Voice:	a. Do children blow out candles at birthday parties?
	b. Do the bride and the groom cut the cake together?
	c. Do people have fireworks at New Year?
	d. Do most people christen their babies?
	e. When do people take part in parades?
	f. When do people wear costumes?
	g. What presents do people give to the bride and groom?
	h. Where do people go on honeymoon?
	i. Who gives a speech at a wedding?
	j. When do people celebrate an anniversary?
Presenter:	1:15
	Exercise D2. Listen and check.
Voice:	culture
	civilization
	custom
	called
	costume
	ceremony
	celebrate
	close
Presenter:	1:16
	Exercise D5. Listen and check.
Voice:	Catholic
	cemetery
	circus
	confetti
	Cupid
	create
	clap

Presenter:	1:17
	Exercise E2. Listen and check.
Voice:	a. weigh — rate
	b. death — guest
	c. bride — dies
	d. grave — prayer
	e. born — groom
	f. birth — church
Presenter:	1:18
	Exercise F1. Listen to the conversations.
	Conversation 1
A:	When were you born?
B:	In 1991.
A:	So you're 20?
B:	Actually, I'm 21.
A:	Are you married?
B:	Yes, I am.
A:	When did you get married?
B:	In 2010.
A:	Do you have any children?
B:	Yes. A baby boy.
A:	When was he born?
B:	In January.
Presenter:	**Conversation 2**
A:	What does your father do?
B:	He's dead, actually.
A:	Oh, I'm sorry.
B:	Thanks.
A:	When did he die?
B:	In 2009.
A:	How old was he?
B:	He was 63.
A:	What happened?
B:	He had a heart attack.
Presenter:	1:19
	Exercise F2. Listen and repeat.
	[REPEAT OF 1:18]

Presenter: 1:20
Unit 2: They Made Our World
Lesson 1: Listening
Exercise C2. Listen. Predict the next word. Then complete the *Accidents p.a.* **and** *Order* **columns.**

Lecturer: What is the safest method of transport? Actually, we can't answer that question before we answer another one. How can we measure safety? One way is to look at the number of accidents for each method. In America in 2002, the largest number of accidents involved [PAUSE] cars. There were 2,378,000 car accidents. In second place, we have accidents involving [PAUSE] pedestrians, that is, people walking near roads or crossing roads. There were 77,000 accidents involving pedestrians. Then, at number three, we have accidents involving [PAUSE] bicycles. There were 58,000 accidents involving cyclists. That's slightly more than accidents involving [PAUSE] motorbikes – the figure there was 54,000. Buses were much safer in this way of measuring. There were only 17,000 bus accidents, but that's still more than twice the number of [PAUSE] boat or ship accidents – 8,000. Finally, we have very small numbers for [PAUSE] trains and planes. Only 3,000 accidents involved trains, and 1,700 involved planes.

Presenter: 1:21
Exercise D. Listen to part of the talk again.

Lecturer: What is the safest method of transport? Actually, we can't answer that question before we answer another one. How can we measure safety? One way is to look at the number of accidents for each method.

Presenter: 1:22
Exercise E3. Listen and check your ideas.

Lecturer: How can we measure transport safety? One way is to look at the number of accidents for each method. Another way is to look at the number of deaths by each method. Do more people die each year in car accidents or plane crashes, for example? We could look at the distance that people travel by each method each year. For example, people travel much longer distances by car than by bicycle, so we could measure the deaths per passenger kilometre. Finally, we could consider the chance of having a fatal accident – the chance of dying when travelling by each method. There aren't many plane crashes, but when a plane crashes, most passengers die. On the other hand, there are millions of car accidents every year, but in most cases, nobody dies.

Presenter: 1:23
Exercise F2. Listen for information about your method. Complete the remaining three columns in Table 1.

Lecturer: So, there are four main ways to measure transport safety. We know about accidents. What about the figures for the other ways? Firstly, let's look at deaths per annum. Again, cars are the most dangerous method of transport. There were 40,000 deaths in 2002 in car accidents. In second place were pedestrians. There were 5,307 deaths of pedestrians. Motorcyclists were in third place, but a long way behind. Two thousand, one hundred and six people died in accidents involving motorcyclists. Less than half that number died in train accidents. The actual figure was 1,096. Cyclists and ship passengers had very similar results – 813 people died in cycling accidents, and 819 in boating or shipping accidents. Fewer plane passengers died – 635. Finally, what about bus passengers? Only 17 people died on buses in the US in 2002.

Another way to measure transport safety is to look at deaths per kilometre. We measure deaths per billion passenger kilometres. When we measure transport safety in this way, we have a new number one. It is motorcyclists. There were 112 deaths per billion passenger kilometres by motorcyclists in the US in 2002. Pedestrians were in second place – 49 deaths, and cyclists third at 41 deaths. Car accidents are in fourth place by this measure – only 2.8 deaths per billion passenger kilometres. Trains caused 0.9 deaths per billion kilometres. Then we have some very small numbers – ships 0.04, buses 0.06 and planes 0.02.

Finally, what is the actual chance of dying during your lifetime in a particular kind of transport accident? When we measure this way, a low figure is bad. I mean, if you have a 1 in 2 chance, that's very bad. If you have a 1 in 2,000 chance, the method's much safer. So, the figures – you have the biggest chance of dying as a pedestrian – 1 in 612. Next, we have car accidents – 1 in 869. Motorbikes are in third place – 1 in 1,159. Cyclists are in less danger – they have 1 chance in 4,857 of dying. For ship accidents, the figure's 1 in 9,019. For plane accidents, it's 1 in 20,015, and for bus accidents, 1 in 86,628. The safest way to travel, according to this measure, is by train. The chance of dying in a train accident is just 1 in 133,035. So, the next time you travel, stop for a moment and think about how safe you are.

Presenter: 1:24

Lesson 2: Speaking
Exercise B. Listen to two conversations.
Conversation 1
Policeman: So, what happened?
Cyclist: I was riding my bike along this road. The door of a car suddenly opened and I hit it. I fell off my bike.
Policeman: Are you all right?
Cyclist: I hurt my arm, but I don't think it's broken.
Driver: I'm so sorry. I was thinking about my appointment. I was late, you see.
Policeman: Late?
Driver: Yes, I was late to see the doctor. I didn't look in the mirror before I opened the door.

Conversation 2
Policeman: So, what happened?
Driver 1: I stopped at the red light. The car behind didn't stop. He went into the back of my car.

Driver 2:	I'm sorry. I was …		A:	How was the journey?
Policeman:	Were you talking on your cellphone?		B:	Fine.
			A:	Oh, good.
Driver 2:	No, I was …			
Driver 1:	Yes, he was. He was talking on his phone and he didn't see the red light.	Presenter:	1:29 Exercise F2. Listen again and complete the conversations. [REPEAT OF 1:28]	
Policeman:	Is that true?			
Driver 2:	Well, yes. I was talking on my phone, but I was looking at the road too.	Presenter:	1:30 **Unit 3 Media and Literature** **Lesson 1: Listening** Exercise A2. Listen and match each extract with one of the posters.	
Policeman:	So, why did you hit the car in front then?			

Presenter: 1:25
Exercise D. Listen to Conversation 1 again.
[REPEAT OF 1:24, Conversation 1]

Presenter: 1:26
Exercise E2. Listen and check.
[REPEAT OF 1:24, Conversation 2]

Presenter: 1:27
Exercise F1. Listen to both conversations again.
[REPEAT OF 1:24]

Presenter: 1:28
Lesson 3: Vocabulary and Pronunciation
Exercise F1. Listen to two conversations. Answer the questions.
Conversation 1
A: Did you drive here?
B: Yes, I did.
A: What was the traffic like?
B: It was terrible!
A: Oh dear!

Conversation 2
A: How did you get here?
B: I came by train.

Voice: 1 In this kind of film, people often go on a journey. They must find something or someone. There are many dangers along the way. Sometimes, they are in a difficult situation and they are in danger of dying.
2 In this kind of story, there is a mystery. Someone is dead and the question is *Who did it?* The main character is a policeman or a private detective.
3 This kind of film makes you frightened. People do frightening things, or suddenly appear and make you jump.
4 This kind of film is set in the past. There are often kings or queens and famous events from history.
5 This kind of story has drawings. The drawings move. Nowadays, the drawings are usually made by computer.
6 This kind of story is often very simple. One person loves another person, but for some reason, they cannot be together. The idea is very simple, but very popular.
7 This kind of story is set in the future. There are often spaceships and people from other planets.

Sometimes, people from the Earth go to another planet, sometimes people from another planet come to the Earth.
8 This kind of story makes you laugh. People do funny things or say funny things.

Presenter: 1:31
Exercise B2. Listen to a research report. Predict the next word when the recording stops. Then complete Table 1.

Researcher: I'm doing research into reading habits in English. I wanted to find out the most popular types of books in the English [PAUSE] language. I looked for information in libraries and on the [PAUSE] Internet. On the website of *The Guardian* newspaper, I found a list of best-selling paperback books for the year [PAUSE] 2002. I looked at the top 50 books in the list and I put them into separate categories – *crime*, *adventure*, [PAUSE] *horror*, etc. Most of the categories are novels, but there are also [PAUSE] *biographies*, or life stories, and *autobiographies* – life stories written by the people themselves. There is also the category *other*, which means [PAUSE] true stories, cookery books, etc. If you look at Table 1, you will see my [PAUSE] results. I found that two types of novel were far more [PAUSE] popular than the rest. In fact, these two types appear 31 times in *The Guardian* list of the first [PAUSE] 50 bestsellers. In other words, they account for over 60 [PAUSE] % of the total. In first place, with 17 out of 50 titles, that's 34%, is [PAUSE] crime novels. Second, with only three fewer titles, we have [PAUSE] love stories. In equal third place, with four titles each, are [PAUSE] science fiction, autobiography and comedy novels. Just behind those three types we have [PAUSE] historical novels with three titles, then [PAUSE] horror and other with two, and finally [PAUSE] adventure and biography with one each.

Presenter: 1:32
Exercise C1. Listen. Make notes in your notebook under the following headings: *Date, Name and country, Number, Age, Tasks 1 and 2.*

Voice: I am going to talk about some research into types of films. In 1996, an American psychologist, Dr Stuart Fischoff – that's Stuart – S-T-U-A-R-T – Fischoff – F-I-S-C-H-O-F-F – did some research into films. He talked to 560 people in the USA. There were 264 men and 296 women. They were between 15 and 83 years old. He asked them to put different types of film in order – with 1 as their favourite. He also asked them to name their favourite film of all time. We can see some of the results of the research in the tables on the screen.

Presenter: 1:33
Exercise C2. Listen. Which word in the tables below does the speaker explain? What is the explanation?

Voice: I must explain one word in these tables. The word is *drama*. Dr Fischoff used traditional categories for film types: love story, science fiction, crime, etc., but he also made a special category called drama. A drama is usually a story at the theatre, but Dr Fischoff used this name for a particular type of film. In drama films, people have a problem and they try to solve it. Sometimes there's a crime in a drama story, but it isn't the main point of the story. Sometimes love is part of a drama film, but it isn't the main part. In most cases, the problem is actually with the people. Dramas teach us about life. Dr Fischoff found that a lot of popular films were dramas, not just crime stories, love stories, and so on.

Presenter: 1:34
Exercise D1. Listen and complete Table 1.

Voice: Dr Fischoff asked the first question to all 560 people: *Can you put these types of film in order of preference, for example, if you like love stories the most, put 1.* The results are in Table 1. He found that drama films were the most popular. In second place were adventure films and in third, sci-fi. Love stories were next and then comedy films in fifth place. In sixth place were cartoons, followed by horror films. Surprisingly, crime stories were in eighth and last place.

Presenter: 1:35
Exercise D2. Listen and complete Table 2 or Table 3.

Voice: Dr Fischoff then asked the second question: *Can you name your favourite film of all time?* The results for women are in Table 2, and for men in Table 3. Not surprisingly, love stories came top for women. Thirty one per cent of women named love stories as their favourite type of film compared with only 4% of men. In second place for women were drama films. Twenty-three per cent chose this type. For men, drama films were top, with 32% saying it was their favourite film type. Science fiction and adventure films were in equal second place for men, with 28% choosing both types. Women put science fiction third – 16 per cent chose this type of film – and adventure fourth – 15% chose this type. Cartoons were next for both men and women, but with only 4% saying it was their favourite film type. Horror, comedy and crime stories got no result at all for either sex. None of the men or women chose these types of films as their favourite.

Presenter: 1:36
Lesson 2: Speaking
Exercise B. Listen to a conversation. Which film are they talking about?

Voice 1: So what's your favourite film of all time?
Voice 2: Mm, I think it's probably [BEEP].
Voice 1: What type of film is it?
Voice 2: Well, it's a historical drama, but I guess it's an action film too.
Voice 1: What happens?
Voice 2: It's set in Roman times. A soldier becomes a slave. Then he becomes a [BEEP]. He becomes the greatest [BEEP] because he's so brave.
Voice 1: Who's in it?
Voice 2: The main character's Russell Crowe.
Voice 1: Oh, really. I like him. How does the film end?
Voice 2: I'm not going to tell you. Watch it!
Voice 1: Perhaps I will.

Presenter:	1:37 Exercise C2. Listen again and check. Write the questions into the spaces. [REPEAT OF 1:36]
Presenter:	1:38 Exercise C3. Listen again. Then practise the conversation in pairs. [REPEAT OF 1:37]
Presenter:	1:39 **Lesson 3: Vocabulary and Pronunciation** Exercise B1. Listen. What do the underlined words have in common? a.
Voice 1:	It's a fantastic film. Go and see it.
Voice 2:	I went swimming in the sea last week. b.
Voice 1:	Kim Basinger played the role of Eminem's mother in *8 mile*.
Voice 2:	I had a cheese roll for lunch.
Presenter:	1:40 **Unit 4: Sports and Leisure** **Lesson 1: Listening** Exercise B. Listen and match each speaker with one of the pictures.
Speaker 1:	I don't think you can really call this a hobby. I mean, everyone does it or nearly everyone, anyway. Some people spend four or five hours every day doing it, even when there's nothing they really want to watch.
Speaker 2:	This hobby is probably most popular with young boys and men. They like making aeroplanes or ships. I don't think many women enjoy doing this.
Speaker 3:	In the past, I think this was more of a woman's hobby. Perhaps, it wasn't really a hobby at all – more like housework. Now, people – men <u>and</u> women – think of it as a hobby and there are lots of TV shows telling you how to make something delicious.
Speaker 4:	I guess this is a popular hobby, but mainly for older people. My mum and dad spend hours outside planting something or watering something. Personally, I think it's a bit boring.
Speaker 5:	This is a very popular outdoor hobby in lots of countries. I don't think it's really a sport – I mean, you can't win or lose. I think men enjoy this more than women. Fathers like to do it with their sons. I think a lot of men do it to get out of the house and escape from the family.
Speaker 6:	I think this is still a popular hobby, even if, nowadays, everything is digital and made easy. Lots of people still like to have a conventional camera and be creative with the pictures they take.
Speaker 7:	People collect all sorts of things. Stamps and coins are very common, but people collect unusual things like teddy bears. I heard a story about a man collecting car number plates.
Speaker 8:	This is a very creative hobby and it's popular with boys and girls equally. At school, children start learning the piano or violin and then as teenagers, the guitar or perhaps drums.
Presenter:	1:41 Exercise C. Listen to the introduction to a talk about hobbies.
Lecturer:	In the modern age, people have a lot of free time or leisure time –

that's time not working. Certainly, more people have more free time than they did a hundred years ago. Then, only rich people had leisure time, while ordinary people worked very long hours. So, how do people fill this leisure time? Well, there are hundreds of different ways. Many people like simple pleasures like reading or listening to music, and a lot of people watch television. Some people have a more specific hobby and this is what I'm going to talk about. I see a hobby as a free-time activity that's creative. I mean, a hobby is a free-time activity that involves making something, or at least seeing some kind of end result.

Presenter: 1:42
Exercise D. Listen to the rest of the lecture.

Lecturer: Sometimes it's easy to see the result of a hobby. For example, in model-making, there's a model at the end of the process – perhaps a plane or a ship. Model-makers probably get more pleasure from making the model than they get from looking at the model or playing with it. That's why they soon start making another model. Photography is another very creative hobby. In photography, there's a photograph, of course, but there's also a collection of favourite photographs. These are perhaps in an album or, nowadays, stored on a computer. Technology – digital photography especially – is making photography seem easy, but many people still enjoy using a conventional camera and getting the best possible image.
Now, DIY – Do-It-Yourself – is another popular hobby. Sometimes with DIY there's a clear result. Perhaps people make a table or a cupboard. Most DIY, however, is simply repairing something – repairing a broken door, doing some electrical work or painting a room, for example. You're still making something, though. You're making the lights work, or you're making the room look nicer. Gardening is similar to Do-It-Yourself, in some ways. You make a space look more beautiful. It's also creative because you look after something and help it to grow. But what about collecting? Can we say that collecting is really a hobby? What are you making? Stamp collectors don't make stamps, coin collectors don't make coins. But they do create something. They make a collection. They put their stamps or coins in an album and they organize it, in alphabetical order by country.

Presenter: 1:43
Exercise E. Listen again.
[REPEAT OF 1:42]

Presenter: 1:44
Lesson 2: Speaking
Exercise D. Listen to the man talking about his hobby.

Voice: OK, I'm going to give you my talk about fishing. Fishing is my favourite activity. It's my hobby. I go fishing every week. In summer, I go two or three times a week. I started when I was six years old with my father. Err ... I say *fishing* because that's a word you all know, but really it's called *angling*. Fishing is catching fish, any kind of catching fish. That can be large commercial fishing with very big nets, for example. Angling is fishing as a *leisure* activity or as a hobby. You spell that A-N-G-L-I-N-G. OK, so why do I like angling? It makes me happy and it makes me feel good. It makes me relax. Fishing in a lake or a river is very relaxing. Fishing in the sea is more exciting. I really enjoy all types.

Angling isn't a very expensive hobby, but you need various equipment. Of course, you need a rod – perhaps, two or three rods. At the moment, I have seven rods – I buy a new rod every year. In the picture, you can see my rod for river fishing. I didn't bring a rod to show you because they're too big to take on the bus! OK, on the rod is the reel. I have a reel here for you to see. It's like a wheel. You turn it to make the line go out or to pull the line back in. I can put different reels on different rods. I have five different reels now – this is just one of them. Of course, next, you must have the hooks if you want to catch a fish. I have a few hooks here to show you. You can see they're different shapes and different sizes. The big hook is for sea fishing – perhaps to catch a tuna, or even a shark. Finally, you need bait. I have to buy bait every month. I have some bait to show you in this tin. Let me just open it. These are maggots – that's M-A-G-G-O-T-S. They're like little worms. Some people don't like them! There are other things we use as bait, for instance small insects and sometimes, just bread. With sea fishing, it's common to use a small fish as bait. Sometimes we throw fish into the sea to make the bigger fish come to the boat.

Now, in river fishing, I often use a fly. That's not a real fly. It's a fly made of metal. It has bright colours, and river fish like these colours. Here are some flies. You can pass them around. With river angling, you also need a net. When you catch a fish, you take it off the hook and put it in the net in the river. At the end of the day, you release the fish back into the water. Sometimes, with sea fishing, I keep the fish to eat. I take a very big fish to a local restaurant.

So, to summarize – I enjoy angling because I find it very relaxing and exciting. I love casting the line and waiting. Then, when I feel a fish, it's very exciting. For me, I'm happiest when I'm reeling in a big fish.

Presenter: 1:45
Exercise D3. Listen again as you read the tapescript.
[REPEAT OF 1:44]

Presenter: 1:46
Lesson 3: Vocabulary and Pronunciation
Exercise F1. Listen and count the syllables.
Voice: favourite
gardening
comfortable
vegetable
chocolate
different

Presenter: 1:47
Exercise F3. Listen again and tick the stress pattern for each word in the table. Then practise saying them.
[REPEAT OF 1:46]

Presenter: 1:48
Exercise F5. Listen and check. Then practise saying these adjectives.

Voice: bored
frightened
surprised
amazed

Presenter: 1:49
Unit 5: Nutrition and Health
Lesson 1: Listening
Exercise B. Listen. Write each food the speaker describes in your notebook.

Voice: 1 People eat this all over the world, but especially in China, Japan and India. People usually eat it with some kind of meat or vegetables.
2 You put this in tea or coffee to make it taste sweet. Some people put it on cereal.
3 This is two pieces of bread with something in the middle, perhaps meat or cheese.
4 These are small pieces of potato fried in oil. People eat them with fish or burgers. Some people eat them every day, but they're not very healthy.
5 Some people say they're fruit. Some people say they're vegetables. They're soft and round and bright red. People eat them in a salad.

Presenter: 1:50
Exercise E3. Listen and check. When the lecturer pauses, say the next word.

Lecturer: At one time, people only ate fresh food and cooked food very quickly. They couldn't keep it for more than [PAUSE] one or two days. But, today, we have two things in our homes to help us keep [PAUSE] fresh food and cooked food. Firstly, we have the [PAUSE] refrigerator – of course, most people just call it a fridge nowadays. In 1856, an Australian called James Harrison produced the first refrigerator – a box with a constant temperature of around [PAUSE] four degrees centigrade. Secondly, we have [PAUSE] plastic wrapping for food. In 1933, an American called Ralph Wiley discovered PVC. After the Second World War, people began to use it to wrap [PAUSE] fresh food and cooked food. Fridges and plastic wrapping mean we can keep fresh food and cooked food for quite a long [PAUSE] time.

Presenter: 1:51
Exercise F3. Listen to the next part of the talk and check.

Lecturer: So, how long can we keep fresh food and cooked food for? Well, for some things, there is really no limit, if we keep them in a cool, dry place. Salt, for example, and coffee and tea. At the other end of the scale, we can only keep cooked meat and fish for one day in a refrigerator and we must wrap it.

Presenter: 1:52
Exercise F4. Listen to the final part and complete the table.

Lecturer: We can keep fresh meat and fish for longer, two days for fish, three to four days for meat. Vegetables also keep for three to four days, cooked rice keeps a little longer, four to five days. Milk keeps for five days, while bread, butter and soft cheese keep for about a week, seven days. Hard cheese, by the way, is different. It keeps for up to three months, that is, 90 days. Eggs keep in a refrigerator for quite a long time, three weeks, or 21 days. Finally, jam and potatoes keep for six months or 180 days.

Presenter: 1:53

Lesson 2: Speaking

Exercise D. Listen to some students.

Extract A

S1: So, what information stands out when you look at this figure?

S2: Well, over half of all cases of food poisoning are in restaurants.

S1: Yes, I noticed that, too. I was quite surprised. Fewer people get food poisoning at home. I guess people at home are more hygienic than people working in restaurants.

Extract B

S2: So, what about this figure? Did you notice anything in particular?

S1: Well, cases of food poisoning decreased over the complete period. However, they increased again at the end of the period.

S2: Yes, that's true. Why was there a dramatic rise in 2001? Why was there a sharp fall the next year?

S1: I have no idea. Perhaps, there was a specific problem, you know, like E. coli a few years ago.

Extract C

S1: It's obvious. The number of cases of E. coli decreased over the period, while the number of cases of salmonella increased.

S2: Yes, the increase was gradual from 2006 to 2009. Then there was a sharp rise in 2010.

Presenter: 1:54

Exercise E2. Listen again and check. Write in the missing words. [REPEAT OF 1:53]

Presenter: 1:55

Lesson 3: Vocabulary and Pronunciation

Exercise C2. Listen and check.

M: So, what do we need?

F: Well, we're making bolognaise and pasta. We certainly need some meat.

M: OK, how much?

F: It's for four people, so quite a lot. Perhaps about two kilos.

M: OK, let's take this pack. It's 2.2 kilos. Do we need to buy pasta?

F: I don't think so. There's quite a lot at home. I bought some a few days ago.

M: What about vegetables?

F: Yes, we need tomatoes, onions and mushrooms.

M: Fresh tomatoes or in a tin?

F: Tinned tomatoes are best for bolognaise.

M: So, how many tins?

F: Let's get three.

M: OK, where are the fresh vegetables?

F: Over here.

M: Right, how many onions do we need?

F: A few, um … three or four, I guess.

M: OK, and mushrooms?

F: We need quite a lot of mushrooms. This pack looks about right. Oh, we need olive oil, too.

M: I think we've got some at home.

F: No, there's only a little in the bottle. We need some more.

M: OK, where can we find that, then?

F: I think it's next to …

Presenter:	**1:56**	9	Hard cheese keeps in a refrigerator for only a few days.
	Exercise E3. Listen and check.	10	Taking regular exercise is good for your heart.
M:	So, what do we need?		
F:	Well, we're making bolognaise and pasta. We certainly need some meat.	Presenter:	**2:2**
M:	OK, how much?		**Exercise C. Listen to the first part of a radio interview. Answer the questions in pairs.**
F:	It's for four people, so quite a lot. Perhaps about two kilos.	Journalist:	Good morning and welcome to *Entertainment Plus*. Today, I'm talking to the manager of a cinema. That's The Picture House cinema in York. Hello, Steve.
M:	OK, let's take this pack. It's 2.2 kilos. Do we need to buy pasta?		
F:	I don't think so. There's quite a lot at home.		
		Manager:	Good morning, George.
Presenter:	**2:1**	Journalist:	Steve – I've got a few questions I'd like to ask about the people who come to your cinema.
	Review		
	Lesson 1: Listening	Manager:	No problem. I like talking about our films and the people who come to watch them.
	Exercise A. Listen to some sentences about the topics you learnt about in Units 1–5. Mark them true or false.		
		Journalist:	So, do different people come to see different films?
Voice:	1 Most weddings in India are quite small. There are only a few guests.	Manager:	Yes, certainly. People come here to see all kinds of films.
	2 It is traditional for the groom to put the ring on the third finger of the bride's right hand.	Journalist:	What films do you show?
		Manager:	Well, as you know, we're a small, independent cinema so we don't show the big Hollywood blockbusters. We never show action movies. People can go to the big cinemas to see them. We show less commercial films – films people may not know about. Last month we showed eight films.
	3 Driving a car or riding a motorbike is more dangerous than travelling by train.		
	4 There are very few plane crashes, but when there is a plane crash, the chances of surviving are very small.		
		Journalist:	And you only have one screen?
	5 Most people, both men and women, usually say that crime stories are their favourite type of film.	Manager:	That's right. Most big cinemas have three or four screens.
		Presenter:	**2:3**
	6 Sherlock Holmes was a detective in the short stories by Sir Arthur Conan Doyle.		**Exercise D. Listen to the rest of the interview and complete Table 1.**
	7 Most people have more leisure time now than they did a hundred years ago.	Journalist:	So, what kind of films did you show?
	8 Digital cameras are making photography too easy. People don't enjoy taking photographs any more.	Manager:	Well, we had an old silent film, in black and white, a love story …

	erm two thrillers, a crime story … er a science fiction film and two foreign language films.
Journalist:	Who came to see them?
Manager:	The audience for the silent film was mostly students from the Art College in town. They were the biggest group of people for the foreign language films, too. We show foreign language films in the original language, with subtitles in English.
Journalist:	What films were they?
Manager:	One was a Korean film called *Old Boy*. The other was *Nicotina*. That's a Mexican film. It's very good.
Journalist:	Tell me more about the audiences.
Manager:	We get a lot of couples – men and women – for a love story. Mostly women come to see thrillers. I think women like to be frightened more than men.
Journalist:	Is it the same for crime films, too? Is it mostly women?
Manager:	Yes, but older women. We get quite a few men as well, but older. So I'd say older people like crime. Perhaps they like to guess who did it – they like a mystery.
Journalist:	How about science fiction? Who likes that?
Manager:	Men, usually. We get a younger audience for a modern science fiction film. Older people come to see the old science fiction films we show. But it's still more men than women.
Journalist:	What about you? What kind of films do you watch?
Manager:	Ah! I work in a cinema because I love films. In my free time, I watch films, too! I watch a comedy on DVD with my family. Now that's entertainment!

Presenter:	2:4
	Exercise G. Listen to the introduction to a lecture about diet.
Lecturer:	The title of my talk today is 'diet and health'. I'm going to compare the diet of the Japanese with the diet of the Western world. I should say that by 'the Western world', I mean Europe and the Americas.
Presenter:	2:5
	Exercise H. Listen to the first part of the lecture. Mark the sentences true or false.
Lecturer:	So, to start with, a western diet is high in fat. In the West, we eat a lot of meat – a lot more meat than our grandparents did. We eat a lot of chicken, for example, because it's cheaper than in the past. It's lower in fat than red meat, such as beef and lamb, but it still has more fat than we actually need. When we eat more than we need to, we add to our body weight. The fat stays with us and some of it remains in our blood. Our heart needs to work harder to use it. On the other hand, in Japan, people eat a lot less meat. They get their protein mainly from fish and beans. Both of these foods are low in fat. The Japanese have fewer heart attacks than people in western countries. This is the reason: in Japan, people don't usually eat bread, so they have no need to eat butter. In fact, in Eastern countries generally, people eat fewer dairy products – milk, cheese, butter and so on. In the West, we eat a lot – probably too much – of these foods. This is another reason why we have such a large amount of fat in our diet. Now, I'm going to go on to talk

about some of the changes that are happening …

Presenter: 2:6
Exercise I. Listen to the second part of the lecture. Complete the notes. Use one or two words in each space.

Lecturer: For the last part of my talk, I want to look at the changes that are taking place in the diet of people in both the West and the East. These changes are happening for a number of reasons, mostly economic. As countries become richer, people spend more money on more food. However, more food doesn't mean that people are eating better. In Japan these days, people are eating more meat. It's now very easy to find fast food, like hamburgers and hotdogs. In some places, it's easier to find fast food than it is to find traditional raw fish.

Unfortunately, as the Japanese eat more hamburgers, they also eat more bread. In many Western countries, doctors want us to eat less meat, or to choose healthier meat with less fat. People in the West are also eating less fish than they did. There is a reduction in fishing and the price of fish in the markets is higher. To replace fish in our diet, Western people are eating more convenience food – more hamburgers and pizzas, as well as food we just need to heat in the microwave. These meals are high in fat, contain too much salt and are generally not healthy.

Presenter: 2:7
Lesson 2: Speaking
Exercise G2. Listen and check your answers.
Conversation 1
A: Do most people get married in church in your country?
B: Yes. People are not always religious, but they still like a church ceremony.
A: Do most people have a traditional white wedding?
B: Oh yes. The bride usually wears a white dress.
A: What happens after the church ceremony?
B: Well, …

Conversation 2
A: Did you fly?
B: Yes, I did.
A: How was the flight?
B: It wasn't very good, actually …

Conversation 3
A: Who's your favourite film character of all time?
B: Err, that's a difficult question. I think it's probably Darth Vader, you know, in *Star Wars*.
A: Oh, really? He's a bad character.
B: Yes, I find heroes a bit boring. What about you?
A I …

Conversation 4
A: What do you like doing in your free time?
B: Well, I like reading and listening to music, but I guess my real hobby's surfing.
A: Really? How often do you go surfing?
B: Every week in the summer. We drive to the beach. Last year, I went surfing in Hawaii too. What about you? What's …

Conversation 5

A: So, what do we need for this omelette?
B: Well, we need eggs.
A: OK, how many?
B: Well, it's for three people, so let's say four.
A: Do we need milk?
B: Yes, but just a little. We mix that with the eggs.
A: OK, then …

Presenter: 2:8

Lesson 3: Vocabulary and Pronunciation

Exercise E2. Listen and check.

Voice:
1 go   role
2 custom   love
3 bride   pilot
4 death   men
5 safe   favourite
6 fast   laugh
7 cartoon   group
8 research   journey
9 found   now
10 sport   water

Presenter: 2:9

Exercise F2. Listen and check.

Voice:
1 ceremony
2 anniversary
3 celebrate
4 population
5 comfortable
6 competition
7 adventure
8 historical
9 literature
10 photography
11 dramatic
12 ingredients

Presenter: 2:10

Lesson 6: Portfolio

Exercise B. Listen. Which activity is the speaker talking about?

Voice: I'm going to talk to you about an activity and tell you why I think you should try it. Now, this activity has a few different names. The most common name is *caving*. It's called that because it's all about discovering caves – underground caves. In the United States, people often call it *spelunking* – that's S-P-E-L-U-N-K-I-N-G. I have no idea where that word comes from. In the United Kingdom, people usually call the activity *potholing* – that's P-O-T-H-O-L-I-N-G. I guess the *holing* part of the name comes from the word *hole*. The activity involves going down some very dark underground holes. I'm going to call the activity *caving* from now on – that makes things easier.
So what do cavers do? Well, they explore underground systems of tunnels and caves. It's very exciting, especially when you find a new cave. I mean a cave nobody else knows. You and your friends are the first people to find it. People say it's dangerous. Well, yes, it's probably more dangerous than most other hobbies, but if you take care, you'll be safe. I like it because it's a little dangerous. I think that makes it exciting. I'm sometimes frightened when a tunnel's full of water. I mean, perhaps the tunnel goes from a lake in one cave to another lake in another cave. You need to swim through the tunnel. It's very dark! I also think you should do this activity because it's very sociable. You work as a team. You help each other and you learn to trust people in dangerous situations.

You make a lot of friends. Another reason to do this activity is that it's not expensive like skiing or scuba diving. You don't need a lot of equipment and it's not necessary to travel far. You need a helmet, the right clothes and some good strong boots. Perhaps you can buy ropes and so on, but if you are in a club, they will have that type of equipment.

So, to conclude; why should people try caving? Because, it's an adventure and it's very exciting. Don't try caving if you don't like small spaces or if you're afraid of the dark!

Presenter: 2:11
Exercise C. Listen again and complete the notes.
[REPEAT OF TRACK 2:10]

WORKBOOK Transcript

Presenter: 1:1

Unit 1: Culture and Civilization
Listening and Speaking
Exercise A2. Listen to the lecture. Write one or two words into each space.

Lecturer: The wedding ring is a very important symbol of marriage. When someone sees a wedding ring, they know a person is married. They know that a person is not free. Wedding rings have a long and interesting history. The custom of giving a ring started in Ancient Egypt. The civilization started to grow close to the River Nile and the river brought life to the Egyptian people. They made rings from reeds. Reeds are the plants that grow in a river. A ring, of course, is a circle, and a circle is a symbol of eternity – a symbol of something that never ends. This was the symbol of the wedding ring for the Egyptians and it was the same symbol for many cultures later in history. In some cultures, the wedding ring is the second important ring of two rings. In Roman times, the custom of giving an engagement ring started. This was, and still is, a promise of marriage.

A ring was not always only a symbol of love. In some cultures, the ring was part of a fortune. A ring was made of gold or silver and the groom gave the ring to his bride as part of his fortune. Often the groom gave a purse of gold or silver coins to his bride after he gave the ring. A friend of the groom or, in some cases, a friend or maid of the bride, looked after the rings before the wedding. He or she produced the ring at a particular moment during the ceremony. Now we often call that person the 'best man'.

In most cultures, only the wife wore a ring as a symbol of marriage. In the 20th century, it became more common for the husband to also wear a wedding ring in some cultures.

Presenter: 1:2

Exercise A4. Listen again and check.
[REPEAT OF 1:1]

Presenter: 1:3

Exercise B. Listen to sentences from a lecture about birthdays.

Lecturer:
1 A 16th birthday is very important in many cultures because the person becomes an …
2 Some people think an 18th birthday is more important than a 16th birthday. When you are 18, you can …
3 Many people celebrate a 21st birthday as a very important birthday. It is traditionally when parents give a son or daughter the keys to …
4 On an 18th or 21st birthday, people have a big party or go out for a special …
5 Forty is another important birthday in many cultures. People sometimes say that life begins at …

Presenter: 1:4

Exercise B2: Listen and check.

Lecturer:
1 A 16th birthday is very important in many cultures because the person becomes an adult.
2 Some people think an 18th birthday is more important than a 16th birthday. When you are 18, you can vote.

3 Many people celebrate a 21st birthday as a very important birthday. It is traditionally when parents give a son or daughter the keys to the door.

4 On an 18th or 21st birthday, people have a big party or go out for a special dinner.

5 Forty is another important birthday in many cultures. People sometimes say that life begins at 40.

Presenter: 1:5

Exercise C1. Respond to each sentence you hear.

Voice: a. President Barack Obama was born in the Seychelles.
b. The birth rate in Africa is falling.
c. El Dia de Los Muertos is a big festival in Brazil.
d. A bride usually wears a black dress.

Presenter: 1:6

Exercise C2. Listen again and write a response below.
[REPEAT OF 1:5]

Presenter: 1:7

Exercise D2. Listen and check.

A: Are you from Germany?
B: Yes, that's right. How did you know?
A: I heard your accent.
B: Oh, I see. Where are you from?
A: Italy. My name's Marco.
B: Hi, I'm Hans.
A: So, is the lecture in this room?
B: I think so, but I'm not really sure. There aren't many other students here.
A: No, I'm going to ask somebody.
B: OK, I'll wait here.

Presenter: 1:8

Unit 2: They Made Our World Listening and Speaking

Exercise B1. Write information into the first four columns of the table. You can use the same information more than once.

Lecturer: Many famous people have died in transport accidents. Perhaps the most famous is Diana, Princess of Wales. She died in Paris, the capital of France, on 31st August, 1997. She was travelling in a car at nearly 200 kilometres per hour. Photographers were chasing the car on motorcycles. The car crashed when it went into a tunnel. Diana died almost immediately.

Another famous person died in a transport accident in the same city 90 years before. Pierre Curie was a famous physicist. He worked with his wife, Marie, and they discovered radium. On the evening of 19th April, 1906, it was raining heavily. Pierre was crossing the road in Paris when the wheel of a carriage hit him. He died instantly.

T. E. Lawrence was a very famous soldier in the First World War. People called him 'Lawrence of Arabia' because he was in Arabic countries for a long time and spoke Arabic perfectly. He nearly died many times during the war, but he finally died in a motorbike accident in Dorset, England. It was 20 years after the end of the war. It was 13th May, 1935 and Lawrence was going very fast on a small country road. There were two children on bicycles in the road. He swerved to miss them and crashed. He died in hospital six days later.

Dag Hammarskjöld was Secretary General of the United Nations. He received the Nobel Peace Prize for his work. On the 17th September, 1961, he was travelling in a plane to the town of Ndola in Zambia. The plane was about 15 kilometres from the airport. The pilot was flying very low, when it hit a tree. It is possible that Hammarskjöld survived the crash, but he was dead when rescuers found him.

Percy Bysshe Shelley is one of the most famous English poets in history. He moved from England to Italy in 1818. He lived in small town called Lerici near Livorno. On 8th July, 1822, he was sailing home from Livorno in his own boat. There was a terrible storm and the boat sank. Shelley drowned. People on another boat found his body a few days later.

Presenter: 1:9
Exercise C. Listen again. Write notes about each accident in the final column of the table.
[REPEAT OF 1:8]

Presenter: 1:10
Exercise D. Listen to some sentences from the recording. Can you understand the underlined words from the context?

Voice: 1 Photographers were chasing the car on motorcycles.
2 Pierre was crossing the road in Paris when the wheel of a carriage hit him.
3 There were two children on bicycles on the road. He swerved to miss them and crashed.
4 It is possible that Hammarskjöld survived the crash, but he was dead when rescuers found him.
5 There was a terrible storm and the boat sank. Shelley drowned.

Presenter: 1:11
Exercise F. Listen to two conversations. Answer the questions.
Conversation 1
A: Did you fly?
B: Yes, I did. The train journey was going to take eight hours.
A: How was the flight?
B: Very quick and very comfortable. I was in Business Class.
A: Oh good!

Conversation 2
A: How did you get here this morning?
B: On the subway.
A: How was the journey?
B: Terrible, actually. There were no seats.
A: Oh dear.

Presenter: 1:12
Exercise G. Listen again and complete the conversations below.
[REPEAT OF 1:11]

Presenter: 1:13
Unit 3: Media and Literature
Listening and Speaking
Exercise A. Listen to some people talking about the films below. Match the number of the speaker with the film posters.

Voices: 1 It's a love story. It's set in India. It's about a man and the woman he loves.
2 I like the little bird. I think he is really funny. He's funnier than the dog, actually.

3 It's about a superhero. He can do amazing things. He's very strong and he can fly. He can climb tall buildings and see things many kilometres away.
4 It's about poor people in India and how one woman helps babies and children.
5 It's very frightening. Is he trying to kill her? Is she going to kill him? You don't know until the very end.
6 So the ship sinks and a group of people get into the lifeboat. But that's not the end of the story. It's just the beginning.
7 There are three men in the film. They do lots of very silly things and make lots of jokes.
8 You know the basic story. A mad scientist makes a monster from parts of human bodies.

Presenter: 1:14

Exercise D2. Listen and check.

Man: How often do you go to the cinema?
Woman: Once or twice a month.
Man: What sort of films do you like?
Woman: Adventure and science fiction.
Man: What about love stories?
Woman: Yeah, I quite like them.
Man: When did you last go to the cinema?
Woman: A couple of weeks ago.
Man: What did you see?
Woman: It was a comedy, actually.
Man: Was it good?
Woman: Yeah, it was really very funny.
Man: What was it about?
Woman: A group of friends. They go on holiday to South America and lots of silly things happen.
Man: How did it end?
Woman: Oh, they all lived happily ever after, of course.

Presenter: 1:15

Unit 4: Sports and Leisure
Listening and Speaking
Exercise A. Listen to some sentences.

Voices:
1 I watched a horror film last night. I was very …
2 I love old Charlie Chaplin films. They really make me …
3 The final score was 4-4. Everyone was very …
4 When we were in New York, we took a helicopter flight around the city. It was …
5 Tony couldn't carry the box by himself. He wasn't strong …

Presenter: 1:16

Exercise A2. Listen and check.

Voices:
1 I watched a horror film last night. I was very frightened.
2 I love old Charlie Chaplin films. They really make me laugh.
3 The final score was 4-4. Everyone was very excited.
4 When we were in New York, we took a helicopter flight around the city. It was amazing.
5 Tony couldn't carry the box by himself. He wasn't strong enough.

Presenter: 1:17

Exercise B. Listen to some sentences. Tick the correct meaning of the words.

Voices:
1 The bank is on the right, opposite the cinema.
2 The plane will land in about 20 minutes.
3 I work very hard all week, but my weekends are usually free.
4 It was a very interesting talk. I learnt a lot.

5 There's a fly in here. Can you try to let it out the window?
6 There are some good matches on this weekend. Perhaps I'll go and see one.

Presenter: 1:18
Exercise C3. Listen to the lecture. Write one or two words into each space.

Lecturer: We know all about how the Romans built roads and how they had a very strong army, but what about their free time? How did the Romans enjoy the time when they weren't working or fighting? Well, like people today, the Romans enjoyed a range of interests and hobbies.

To start with, they loved playing board games. In museums, we can see the boards, the dice and the counters they played with. Nobody understands the rules, though!

Romans also enjoyed hunting. At that time, many people hunted for necessity, but the Romans hunted for pleasure. They introduced new animals to the countries they occupied so hunting was more enjoyable.

The theatre was very popular. People watched plays and listened to music. The actors and actresses often wore masks to show that they were a good or bad character. The Romans also had enormous amphitheatres. The games and activities that took place in the amphitheatres were violent and cruel. Slaves and prisoners, called *gladiators*, fought each other to the death. Sometimes they fought wild animals like lions and bears. The Romans used chariots in war, but chariot racing was also a very popular leisure activity. Chariot racers became celebrities – like footballers today – and they could become very rich.

Perhaps the most famous of the Romans' leisure activities was relaxing in a hot bath. We can still find these bathhouses around the world. The Romans spent all day at the baths. They did exercises before bathing and then swam afterwards. The baths were important meeting places and rich Romans conducted business as they bathed.

Presenter: 1:19
Exercise D2. Listen and check.
Conversation A
A: Have you got any hobbies?
B: Yes, I make models.
A: What kind of models?
B: Well, I'm interested in cars.

Conversation B
A: What do you do in your free time?
B: I like going to the cinema.
A: What kind of films do you watch?
B: Anything really, but I really like horror films.

Conversation C
A: Do you play any sports?
B: Not much. I play a little tennis.
A: Are you good at it?
B: No, but I like playing.

Conversation D
A: What do you do in the evenings?
B: Not much, I'm usually too tired.
A: So, how do you relax?
B: I watch TV or read a book.

Presenter: 1:20
**Unit 5: Nutrition and Health
Listening and Speaking
Exercise B. Listen to the introduction. Fill in the missing numbers in *Did you know ...?***

Voice: You need food for energy. If you don't eat, you'll get ill. But you must be careful with food, because food can make you ill, too. If food makes you ill, we say it poisons you. In the USA, over 30 million people get food poisoning every year. Nearly 10,000 Americans die from food poisoning every year. So it is a serious problem.

Presenter: 1:21
Exercise C. Listen to the next section. Think about the advice in *Remember!*

Voice: Food will poison you if it has a lot of bacteria in it. Bacteria are tiny living creatures. They get into food and multiply very quickly. Bacteria like warm, wet conditions. They grow best in temperatures between 5 degrees Celsius and 60 degrees Celsius. But bacteria don't like it too hot. They start to die at temperatures of 70 degrees, and at 100 degrees, 99.9% are dead. So, bacteria in food can make you ill. Luckily, it is quite easy to stop bacteria getting into food, or to kill the bacteria in food before you eat. Just follow these simple rules.

Presenter: 1:22
Exercise D. Listen and complete each piece of advice.

Voice: Firstly, bacteria like it hot and they like it wet, so [pause] keep raw food cool and dry. Secondly, bacteria need time to multiply, so [pause] don't keep food for too long. Thirdly, there are bacteria on dirty hands, so [pause] wash your hands before you cook food and, fourthly, of course, wash your hands [pause] before you eat food. Next, bacteria like heat, so they multiply when you start cooking food. However, when the food is really hot – above 75 degrees Celsius – they start to die, so [pause] cook food for long enough. Finally, bacteria multiply as the food cools down, so [pause] eat food soon after cooking.

Presenter: 1:23
Exercise E. Listen and complete the *Fact*.

Voice: Bacteria are all around us – on our hands and in the food before we start to cook it, so be careful. The figures are frightening. One bacterium in food can become 2 million bacteria in just 7 hours in the right conditions.

Presenter: 1:24
**Exercise F3. Listen and check your answers.
Conversation 1**

A: Can I have a ham and salad sandwich, please?
B: White or brown bread?
A: Oh, brown, please.
B: Would you like some mayonnaise?

Conversation 2

A: Would you like some more soup?
B: Just a little. I'm quite full.
A: Here you are.
B: Thanks very much.

Conversation 3

A: What are you cooking? It smells delicious.

B: Fish with tomatoes and black olives.
A: Are you frying the fish?
B: No, I'm baking it in the oven.

Conversation 4
A: Let's go out for dinner this evening.
B: OK. Do you want to try the new Italian place?
A: Yes, why not? I'll book a table for eight.
B: Good idea. If we don't book, we might not get a table.

Presenter: **1:25**
Review
Listening and Speaking
Exercise A1. Number the best word or phrase to complete each sentence. You don't need all the words.

Lecturer: 1 A 16th birthday is very important in many cultures because the person becomes an …
2 There were amazing parades. People were dancing in the …
3 I sometimes get a bit nervous when the plane takes off and then again when it …
4 We watched a great comedy last night. It really made us …
5 When I'm playing tennis, I don't think about anything else. I forget all my …
6 You should put food straight in the fridge if you want to keep it …

Presenter: **1:26**
Exercise A2. Listen and check.

Voice: 1 A 16th birthday is very important in many cultures because the person becomes an adult.
2 There were amazing parades. People were dancing in the street.
3 I sometimes get a bit nervous when the plane takes off and then again when it lands.
4 We watched a great comedy last night. It really made us laugh.
5 When I'm playing tennis, I don't think about anything else. I forget all my problems.
6 You should put food straight in the fridge if you want to keep it fresh.

Presenter: **1:27**
Exercise B1. Respond to each sentence you hear.

Voice: a. People celebrate a golden wedding anniversary after 25 years of marriage.
b. Flying is one of the most dangerous methods of transport.
c. *Romeo and Juliet* is one of the world's favourite crime stories.
d. Smoking makes your clothes smell lovely.

Presenter: **1:28**
Exercise B2. Listen again and write a response below.
[REPEAT OF 1:27]

Presenter: **1:29**
Exercise D2. Listen and check.
A: What time does the film start?
B: I'm not really sure. There are usually advertisements first.
A: I'll ask at the desk.

A: Let's go and see a film tonight.
B: OK, why not? Is there something you want to see?
A: The new Julia Roberts film looks interesting.

A: You study medicine, don't you?
B: Yes. That's right. I'm in my second year.
A: I study literature.

A: I went to a job interview this morning.
B: How was it?
A: Not bad. I think they liked me.
B: Oh good!

A: Does this word mean 'not expensive'?
B: Yes, I think so. I'll check in my dictionary.
A: Thanks.

A: Was your journey OK?
B: Actually, it was terrible. There was a lot of traffic.
A: Oh dear.

Word list

	Unit		Unit
accident (n)	2	crime film (n)	3
action film (n)	3	custom (n)	1
activity (n)	4	cyclist (n)	2
actor (n)	3	dangerous (adj)	2
actress (n)	3	death (n)	1
adventure (n)	3	death rate (n)	1
aeroplane (n)	2	death (n)	2
airport (n)	2	decrease (v/n)	5
amateur (n/adj)	4	die (v)	1
anniversary (n)	1	direct (a film) (v)	3
author (n)	3	director (n)	3
autobiography (n)	3	do-it-yourself (DIY) (n)	4
average (adj/n)	1	drama (n)	3
bag (n)	5	dramatic (adj)	5
be born (v)	1	economical (adj)	2
bicycle (n)	2	enjoy (v)	4
birdwatching (n)	4	equipment (n)	4
birth (n)	1	event (n)	1
birth rate (n)	1	exercise (v/n)	5
birthday (n)	1	expensive (adj)	2
blow out candles (v)	1	fall (v/n)	5
bottle (n)	5	falling population (n)	1
box (n)	5	fast (adj)	2
bus (n)	2	favourite (adj)	3
calories (n)	5	firework display (n)	1
car (n)	2	fireworks (n)	1
cartoon (n)	3	fishing (n)	4
case (n)	5	fly (v)	2
cause (v/n)	5	food poisoning (n)	5
celebrate (v)	1	free time (n)	4
ceremony (n)	1	fresh (adj)	5
character (n)	3	fridge (n)	5
christening (n)	1	funeral (n)	1
collect (v)	4	gardening (n)	4
collecting (v)	4	get married (v)	1
collection (n)	4	gradual (adj)	5
collector (n)	4	growth (n)	1
comedy (n)	3	guest (n)	1
comfortable (adj)	2	happen (v)	1
convenient (adj)	2	hard cheese (n)	5
costume (n)	1	healthy (adj)	5
crash (n/v)	2	historical film (n)	3
creative (adj)	4	hobby (n)	4
crime (n)	3	hobbyist (n)	4

honeymoon (n)	1
horror film (n)	3
inconvenient (adj)	2
increase (v/n)	5
interests (pl n)	4
involve (v)	2
jar (n)	5
journey (n)	2
leisure time (n)	4
life expectancy (n)	1
love story (n)	3
make a speech (v)	1
marriage (n)	1
measure (v)	2
method of transport (n)	2
model-making (n)	4
motorbike (n)	2
motorist (n)	2
notice (v)	5
novel (n)	3
occasion (n)	1
parade (n)	1
passenger (n)	2
pedestrian (n)	2
photography (n)	4
piece (n)	5
play (a part/role) (v)	3
pleasure (n)	4
popular (adj)	4
present (n)	1
professional (n/adj)	4
raw (adj)	5
red meat (n)	5
refrigerator (n)	5
restaurant (n)	5
rise (v/n)	5
rising population (n)	1
role (n)	3
safe (adj)	2
safety (n)	2
scene (n)	3
science fiction (sci-fi) film (n)	3
set (be set in) (v)	3
sharp (adj)	5
significant (adj)	5
slice (n)	5
slow (adj)	2
smoke (v)	5
smoking (n)	5
soap (n)	5
soft cheese (n)	5
speech (n)	1
stamp collecting (n)	4
stand out (v)	5
star-gazing (n)	4
statement (n)	2
take exercise (v)	5
tip (n)	5
toothbrush (n)	5
traffic (n)	2
train (n)	2
uncomfortable (adj)	2
unhealthy (adj)	5
wedding (n)	1
witness (n)	2
wrap (v)	5
wrapping (n)	5